The Story
We Carry
in Our Bones

The Story We Carry in Our Bones

Irish History for Americans

Written by Juilene Osborne-McKnight

Illustrated by Mara Kate McKnight

PELICAN PUBLISHING

2018

First printing, October 2015
Second printing, January 2018

*The word "Pelican" and the depiction of a pelican are
trademarks of Arcadia Publishing Company, Inc., and are
registered in the U.S. Patent and Trademark Office.*

Library of Congress Cataloging-in-Publication Data

Osborne-McKnight, Juilene.
  The story we carry in our bones : Irish history for Americans / written by
Juilene Osborne-McKnight ; illustrated by Mara Kate McKnight.
      pages cm
  Includes bibliographical references and index.
    ISBN 978-1-4556-2533-8 (paperback : alk. paper) — ISBN 978-1-4556-2072-
2 (e-book) 1. Ireland—History. 2. Irish—United States—History. 3. Irish
Americans—History. I. Title.
  DA938.O76 2015
  941.5—dc23
                              2015009436

All photographs by author unless otherwise indicated

Printed in the United States of America

Published by Pelican Publishing
New Orleans, LA
www.pelicanpub.com

Contents

PART IV   IRISH ROOTS AND RISING IRISH: THE IRISH BECOME AMERICAN

Acknowledgments

The one way in which we Irish-Americans have always been rich—even when we were scrabbling and starving—is in our families and our friendships.

Early in our American immigration we were accused of being far too clannish. I am guilty of that, still, and gladly. So thanks go to the following, who helped me every step of the way:

First and always to Thomas Glenn McKnight, my own Scots-Irishman, my *anam cara,* who made the meals and ate them with the computer between us, and carried the cameras on countless shoots in the field, and never tired of listening to me tell it even when he was tired of listening to me tell it. My life would not have been my life without you.

To my daughter Mara Kate McKnight, who drew the gorgeous and complex Celtic illustrations and the whimsical sketches all throughout this book, and to her husband, Seamus Doran, who ran technical interference on every computer and monitor.

To Sarah Nytroe, Ph.D. (history), my dear friend, who read the book carefully, looking for any necessity for citations and for any historical contradictions. All mistakes are mine but many corrections are hers.

To De Sales University for giving me so many Irish travel opportunities, and for too many additional blessings to count. *Go raibh mile maith agat.*

To my agent, Natalia Aponte, with me through so many books.

To my new editor, Nina Kooij, who strikes me as a master of detail; this is a quality I strive for and admire. And to Sally Boitnott, also at Pelican Publishing Company, who fielded all the forms and correspondence with such good humor.

And, of course, to Ireland. *Is Mheiriceánach-Ghaeilge me. Agus bródúil as é. Bródúil.*

Introduction

"Diaspora": it's a lovely word, with its sibilant *s* and its round vowels. It sounds like a long and leisurely journey, but for our Irish ancestors, it was anything but.

"Diaspora" means the dispersion of any people from their traditional homeland. In the case of our Irish ancestors, they were heaved, chased, and starved out of the green hills of Ireland then flung far and wide into an unwelcoming world. At various stages of our history, our ancestors ended up in France as fleeing warriors, in Barbados as captured slaves, in England as the starving homeless, in Australia as debtor deportees, and in Canada and the United States as the largest immigrant influx in our history.

They arrived poor, starving, and uneducated, capable of hard work but unwelcome in most places of employment. Most of them arrived knowing full well that they would never again see their parents or relatives, never again see the soft sky and the sweet green fields of Ireland.

Some saved what they could — a tune on an old fiddle, a story about an ancient member of the clan, a whispered tale about a banshee. Others, desperate to blend into their new surroundings, to lose the stigma of being an Irish immigrant, abandoned the old ways as fast as they could. They worked to get rid of the lovely but limiting brogue, told no stories of Ireland, spoke no words that might invoke their own strangeness. They got their children educated and moved up the American ladder. Sometimes their motto became: "We don't talk about that." At once open and friendly, secretive and select, they moved, as so many immigrants do, to eradicate their past, to become apple-pie Americans.

And yet, even so many generations down, something Irish survived. According to the 2010 census, 35 million Americans consider themselves to be of direct Irish ancestry; add on those who consider themselves Scots-Irish-American and the number stands at 40 million—eight times greater than the population of Ireland itself! There are decided concentrations of these Irish in Boston, New York, Philadelphia, Chicago, and Savannah, but the Irish are ubiquitous in America. We *are* the American diaspora. By now, we are a fascinating mixed bag—a fifty-seven-varieties ethnic group—Irish and Italian, Irish and Scots, Irish and African, Irish and Cherokee-Mohawk-Huron. We have become a quintessentially American world salad. But when asked to define our ancestry on a census or other form, we define ourselves as Irish.

According to Prof. Kevin Kenney of Boston College, we Irish-Americans as an ethnic group are larger, better educated, and higher earning than any other ethnic group in the United States.

We are proud of our success in the framework of American life, but we are also proud of our Irishness. Yet, oftentimes that pride is a little vague. Some of us trot it out on St. Patrick's Day, take it to the parade, wear all the green we can muster, drink a Guinness, and tell a little tale about a leprechaun. Some of us travel to Ireland, attend Irish festivals, and name our children Sean or Meghan, Patrick or Caitlin. Quite a few of us research our family tree, discovering in the process the name of the coffin ship that bore our ancestors over, or the documents that indicate that someone in the family may have departed the homeland on the run.

But we don't really know what that means. How do we fit into the great diorama of Irish history? What is the ancestry that we carry in our bones, even now, even these many generations down the diaspora?

This book is for us. It is not an academic tome that focuses on one battle or one hero or villain. It is not a sociological study. This book is the thing that all Irish-Americans love most. It is a feast—a huge buffet celebration of our whole history, there and here, then and now, heroes and villains, music and stories, joys and sorrows. You can read it cover to cover or dip in again and again. You can focus on our stories or our religions, on our battles there or our battles here, on the wild characters who preceded us or the immigrant characters who forged us a path in this new world.

It has been my great privilege to spend my life teaching Irish history, myth, and literature, to study in Ireland, and to write Irish novels. I offer this book as my gift to my fellow Irish-Americans. I hope that our story surprises and delights you, inspires you, and takes you on a journey home. It's a big story, brothers and sisters, and we are still telling it.

Bail O Dhia ar an obair.
Bless, O God, the work.

The Story
We Carry
in Our Bones

Knock Wood and Light the Pumpkin

Your Ancient Ancestors Are Closer
Than You Think

Part I: Knock Wood and Light the Pumpkin: Your Ancient Ancestors Are Closer Than You Think

1
Prehistoric Ireland:
Megaliths and Mystery

Ancient of Days

People were living in Ireland as early as 6800 B.C., dwelling on a heavily forested island inhabited by wild horses, wolves, and giant deer with twelve-foot antler racks. These early folk used stone tools, farmed, hunted, and gathered. They lived in villages with both circular and rectangular houses. Before 3000 B.C.—earlier than the Great Pyramid Builders of Egypt— they were erecting massive stone structures to honor their dead and celebrate the cosmos.  More than four thousand dolmens (stone arbors or doorways) and megaliths are evidence of a complex civilization that understood science, astronomy, history, and architecture. But who were they? Where did they come from and when? How did they garner their great body of knowledge? Were they the people now known as Celts? The truth is, we simply don't know. They are our most ancient ancestors but they are shrouded in mystery.

Along the Boyne River Valley in County Meath, Ireland, they left us numerous passage graves, graves cut deep into the earth via long tunnels; most astonishing are Newgrange, Knowth, and Dowth. At Newgrange, a long, low passage leads to a central chamber roofed by a corbeled ceiling so perfectly constructed that no rain leaks into the chamber, even after 5,000 years. For generations, the ashes

Ulster

Emain *
Macha

Connacht

Meath *
(Mide)
*

Hill of   Newgrange
Tara

Leinster

Munster

Ancient Ireland

of the venerated dead commingled in a great bowl at the center of the chamber. Obviously, these were people with a highly developed concept of ancestry, of death and life, of passage to a world beyond this world, a passage that opened somewhere in the depths of the earth.

The passage graves are astronomical marvels as well. The lintel above the doorway to Newgrange on the Boyne is perfectly aligned with the sun at winter solstice. For fifteen minutes on that day, golden light inches—then streams—down the long hallway, eventually illuminating the central chamber in its brief, lambent glow. So transcendent is this experience that people from all over the world

The passage grave at Newgrange in the Boyne River Valley. Note the spiraling knotwork on the entrance stone. Similar patterns line the walls inside the passage grave. Most scholars believe the carvings to be deeply religious, the never-ending braids perhaps symbolic of a belief in life after death or in reincarnation. The entire mound uses more than four thousand tons of stone.

The Poulnabrone Dolmen (*Poll na mBron* or "hole of the sorrows") on the Burren in County Clare. Originally these doorways were used as burial chambers, backfilled with dirt and gravel and sometimes covered with grass, but centuries of wind and rain wore them open. When this dolmen was excavated, it contained the remains of twenty-two people, six of them children, none over forty years old, and many with arthritis—evidence that our ancient ancestors must have lived short, hard lives in this windswept stony country.

Dolmens exist everywhere in Ireland: in the midst of the cattle in farmers' fields, on hillsides, and in hollows. Clearly these ancestral people populated the entire island and believed in death as a passageway.

Of course, many legends have arisen surrounding these doorways, including that to pass through them is to pass into the country of the Little People, the "Other" of Irish myth, but much more on those little folk later.

book tickets years in advance, hoping for a cloudless, sunny day in Ireland (that last alone a giant leap of faith). But winter solstice is not required for the full impact of the experience. Deep in the heart of the earth, in absolute silence and palpable darkness, it is possible to intuit the ancient heart of history.

Who Came Before? The Mythology of Prehistory

In the absence of anthropological data about the ancient people of Ireland, myth rushes in to fill the gap. According to the *Leabhar Gabhala*—the Book of Invasions, pronounced *Lauer Gavahla*—which was written down in the eighth century A.D., there were six invasions of ancient Ireland.

- The people of Cesair. According to the myth, Cesair was a female leader whose entire race of people drowned with the exception of Fintan, her consort, who survived as a falcon, eagle, hawk, or salmon, i.e., a shapeshifter. This shapeshifting motif runs through all of the mythological cycle of Irish stories. Disney's *The Sword in the Stone,* in which Merlin changes Arthur into a squirrel and a fish, is a perfect example of this ancient Celtic concept—become another and you will understand how another thinks.

- The Fomorians. Combine *Pirates of the Caribbean* with the Cyclops of Greek myth and you have a relative idea of the Fomorians. They were raiders who lived on Tory Island (Túr Rí, Tower of the King) off the coast of Ireland, having survived, according to legend, the Great Flood. The Fomorians are hideous monsters; their "secret weapon" Balor of the One Eye, a hairy giant with an eye in the middle of his forehead, wields a vicious and deadly club. They were fond of raiding and kidnapping and are the stuff of mythological nightmares.

- The Partholon. According to the myth, they were a race of makers who created ten lakes, nine rivers, and four plains. They built the first guesthouse and dwelling, brewed beer, brought gold and cattle, and created a legal system. They were also the first to fight the aforementioned Fomorians. Unfortunately, the entire race of the Partholon were destroyed by a plague on the first of May, the date that would become the sacred Celtic feast of Beltaine.

- The Nemedians. The awful fate of this supposedly gentle race was that they became tribute slaves of the Fomorians. Each November first—the sacred Celtic feast day of Samhain, or Celtic New Year— the Fomorians demanded two-thirds of all Nemedian produce, as well as two-thirds of their children as slaves. Eventually, the Nemedians revolted; many were killed and survivors fled for the Continent.

- The Firbolg. Some versions of the myth have them arriving on August 1 (Lughnasa) in the captured ships of their Greek slavemasters, accompanied by Gauls and Dumnonii, Celtic tribesmen of France and Britain. The Firbolg settled in the west country of Connacht.

- The Tuatha de Danaan (the tribe of the goddess Danu). These folk become the fabled Little People of Ireland and their gods become the gods of the early Celtic inhabitants of the island; much more on them later.

Eventually, around the year 500 B.C., all of these "races" were

The far south of Ireland at the Ring of Kerry. The Milesians supposedly landed at the Bay of Kenmare. Note the ancient ring fort at the center of the photo.

supposedly supplanted by the Milesians, an actual historical tribe of Iberian Celts from the northwest coast of Spain, at which point "verifiable" Irish history begins. The archeological truth of that arrival, however, is much more complicated, as we will see.

Power Over Time: The Little People of Ireland

Fado, fado: long long ago, there lived in Ireland an ancient race of people who never grew sick, never grew old, and never died, for they held power over time. . . . So begins the ancient myth of the Tuatha de Danaan, the tribe of the goddess Danu. Small and exquisitely beautiful—both the men and women—the de Danaan were nonetheless fully formed humanoid beings, whose diminutive bodies gave off an unearthly glow, a radiant aura variously depicted as blue, gold, or iridescent.

Three legends explain the presence of these Little People in Ireland. All say that they arrived on the first of May (Beltaine, one of the ancient sacred holidays). The first has them arriving from Greece, the second from a wondrous city that disappeared beneath the sea in a great earthquake (evidently the legendary Atlantis), and the third from cloud ships that hovered above the island. Whatever the place of origin or mode of delivery, the Little People never left. In time, they came to be known by a variety of names by the human inhabitants of the island: *An Sidhe* (the Others, pronounced *An Shee*), the Little People, the Shining Folk, the Fair Folk, and the fairies. So they remain, even to this day, but do not think of them as leprechauns, for the Little People of Ireland are much older, much wiser, and much more dangerous than that.

According to the myth, there were people already on the island when the Tuatha de Danaan arrived—the Firbolg, who lived in the west country of Connacht—but the Tuatha de Danaan possessed *draoidheacht,* or magic. They defeated the Firbolg in the First Battle of Mag Tuiread (pronounced *Moy Tirra*) for control of the island, but their battle had a terrible price. Nuada, the chief of the Tuatha de Danaan, lost his arm in the fight. By the laws of the de Danaan, physical imperfection disqualified him from kingship. The tribe selected Bres the Handsome, whose mother was a Danaan but whose father was a Fomorian. Bres turned out to be a disaster. First he lacked generosity, a cardinal sin among the Tuatha de Danaan, and later among the Irish. He did not provide for poets, musicians, and jesters, stinting them on beer and biscuits, which caused the poets to write the first satire against him. (Satire by a poet in ancient Ireland was so dangerous that it could kill its victim or cause him to break out in boils.) Worse, however,  Bres turned traitor and brought the one-eyed Balor and his piratical Fomorians down upon the Tuatha de Danaan.

The de Danaan would have been defeated, but they were assisted by Lugh, the Son of the Light. Young, handsome, and pure of heart, Lugh was at once a carpenter, blacksmith, poet, harper, genealogist, hero, healer, and sorcerer. While he battled the Fomorians with his magical spear, the physicians of the Tuatha de Danaan built for Nuada a magical silver arm, and he rejoined the fight. Together, Lugh and Nuada defeated the Fomorians. Nuada was renamed king, known from that time forward as Nuada Argetlamh (Silver Arm), and the mythical de Danaan became, according to the ancient tales, the dominant race on the island until 500 B.C.

Triumvirates and Trinities

Three was the sacred number in ancient Celtic Ireland. Many gods and rulers were tripartite, one reason why Ireland eventually Christianized so easily (more on that in part 2). Many artifacts display three-headed gods. We do not know the origin of this preoccupation with threes, but among our mythological Little People, two early sets of rulers and the two most powerful god figures are, respectively, triumvirates and trinities.

The myths tell us that the Tuatha de Danaan were ruled for a time by a trilogy of brothers—MacCuill, MacCecht, and MacGreinne. Though we know nothing of them as rulers, the next threesome of rulers were women—Banba, Fodla, and Eriu (Ireland was equal opportunity for both gods and rulers). Eriu gave her name to the island: Eire, Erin, Ireland.

The goddesses of the Tuatha de Danaan were particularly powerful in trinities. The Light Trinity of the Danaan were the three goddesses Brighid, Anu, and Dana. While Anu and Dana are referred to in the myths as the mothers of gods, Brighid is the goddess of all the creative forces— childbirth, mothers, ewes, fire, poetry, blacksmithing. Her feast day was Imbolc, February first. In the most fortunate of households, she left her footprints in the home from the hearth ashes. So powerful was the Brighid archetype that she permuted into Christianity's St. Brighid, and actual early Christian saints such as St. Brigid of Kildare are her namesakes. Irish legends say that she served as a midwife at the birth of Christ.

Equally powerful, however, was the dark trinity of the Morrigu. Composed of three fearsome parts, the Morrigu's "personalities" are Macha, goddess of war; Banbh, goddess of carrion; and Nemhain, goddess of panic and chaos. These three live to cause trouble. When the Celts eventually arrive in Ireland, this trilogy troubles every human hero for hundreds of years. So powerful is this dark trinity that they show up as the Weird Sisters in Shakespeare's *Macbeth* and later, conflated into one woman, they vie for power as Morgan le Fay in the Arthurian myths.

"Banbh, Nemhain, Macha." Eriu addressed them separately with a formal nod. "We of the Triad Council are willing to listen to your wisdom."

"Wisdom is it?" said Macha. She smiled, her lips folding up into a rictus that looked almost painful. "When have any of the Danu considered us wise?"

Eriu resisted swallowing. She looked at them each in turn. Panic rose in her throat when she met the eyes of Nemhain, but she fought it back. Panic is what Nemhain engendered. Everywhere she went, she seemed to be able to draw upon any creature's worst fear, bring it to the surface, strengthen it until the poor victim gibbered in terror, made terrible decisions based upon that panic.

Panic was not what she felt when she regarded Banbh; rather she felt revulsion. It was rumored among her people that Banbh's favorite use of metaphor were as those of carrion feeders, ravens and vultures, birds of darkness who fed on the blood of the fallen.

And then there was Macha, their Primary Sister. She was beautiful, although she in no way resembled the People of the Danu, no nor the Penitents. She was taller, even than her sisters. Her long, black hair floated and shifted in the breeze and her dark almond-shaped eyes gave away nothing, reflected everything. Eriu could see herself in them now, small and pale, her cap of cloudy curls ruffling in the wind, her eyes wide and startled.

However, these trilogies were not the only gods of the de Danaan; others included:

- Dagda—The "good" god, good meaning provider; Dagda is the possessor of a bottomless cauldron filled with porridge
- Boann—Wife of the Dagda and goddess of the Boyne River
- Dian Cecht—God of physicians
- Gobniu—God of blacksmiths
- Aengus Og—God of birds, butterflies, and love
- Ogma—Honey-mouthed god of oratory and sweet speech
- Manannan Mac Lir—God of the sea
- Mongan—Son of Manannan, shapeshifter and god of the beasts

The leprechaun is an Americanized version of the Little People of Ireland, trotted out for St. Patrick's Day and several silly or scary movies. Leprechauns in Irish folklore come much later than the de Danaan and are shoemakers, all male, tricksters, and somewhat irritable. The name may derive from the Irish *leith brogan* (shoemaker) or *lugh chromain* (small or hunchbacked Lugh, a diminution of Lugh Lamfhada, the god of the long spear arm). Rainbows, pots of gold, and lucky shamrocks all come much later and are much less powerful than the magic of the ancient Tuatha de Danaan. Closely related to the leprechauns are cluricaunes, who are little thieves, particularly of the wine and whiskey in family cellars.

The Legend of the Bain Sidhe

"Someone in the family will die soon," your Irish grandmother might have said, shaking her head sadly. "Last night I heard the banshee crying at the window."

You don't have to be Irish to have heard of the banshee. Phrases such as "screaming like a banshee" or "wailing like a banshee" have passed into common American usage. The word *banshee* derives from two Irish Gaelic words, *bean* or *bain* (woman) and *sidhe*, which simply means "of the other." In Celtic mythology, she was a woman of the Little People—the Tuatha de Danaan—who attached herself to one of the major Irish clans. Blessed or cursed with the "Sight," the banshee knew when someone in the clan was about to die and so performs the *caoineadh* (keening) that mourns the death in advance. Many legends agree that she sees this as her honorable duty to the ancient Irish clans. Some versions of the legend have her dressed all in white or silver with long white hair. She can appear as a beautiful young woman or a terrifying hag, but all agree that her mournful lament chills the bones and brings sorrow to the heart.

Gaelic Languages

"Banshee" is not the only Irish-origin word to have traveled to America. We also brought along the words "galore," from the Irish *maith go leor* or good enough, "brogues" for shoes, "colleen" from the Irish *cailin* or girl, "hooligan" from the Irish name O'Houlihan, and the aforementioned "keening" from the Irish *caoineadh*.

There is no single language known as "Gaelic," although most Americans think Gaelic is what we mean by Irish. Instead, there are six distinctive forms of Gaelic languages, some in regular use, others vanishing or vanished from the earth.

Note that the languages are related to each other by color. This is because speakers of each set of three could understand each other,

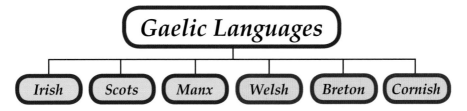

though there would be variations, but a speaker of Irish would not understand a speaker of Welsh or Cornish or vice versa. Why is this? It is believed that the protolanguage of the Gaelic languages arose from the Indo-European language base, but because it moved in waves, two types of Gaelic eventually differentiated themselves. Q-Gaelic or Goidelic was the first wave—those wanderers who arrived on the islands now known as Ireland, England, Scotland, and Wales somewhere between 2000 and 1200 B.C. This form of Gaelic eventually permuted into Irish, Scots, and Manx. The second wave of immigrants spoke P-Gaelic, also called Brythonic, and that language eventually formed as Welsh, Breton, and Cornish.

Currently, Cornish has vanished as a language. Manx all but vanished but has been heroically revived on the Isle of Man. Irish has long been considered a dying language, but there is now a huge effort to revive it.

Irish is the official language of the Republic of Ireland and has been named one of the official languages of the European Union. It is mandatory in all schools, used in various publications and on some radio (Raidio na Gaeltachta) and television programs (Telefis na Gaeltachta, now T4), and used in a ceremonial way in the business of the Dail, or Irish Parliament. The 2011 Irish census found more than 40 percent of the Irish people claiming knowledge of Irish, but estimates are that, in truth, only 3-5 percent of the Irish population speak it as their primary (birth) language and as the language of everyday life.

Many of these people (about 90,000) are located in the Gaeltachta, the Irish-speaking regions of Ireland: Galway, Connemara, Mayo, West Donegal, the Dingle Peninsula, Kerry, and the Aran Islands. An interesting new program called the Scéim Labhairt na Gaeilge pays grants to families with native Irish competency. The Irish government also removed English road and directional signs in the Gaeltachta in an effort to keep those areas purely Irish. This effort has had mixed reactions, as tourists find the Irish-language road signs impenetrable.

Interestingly, however, there is a huge push among Irish Americans to learn the Irish language. Irish-studies programs such as those at Harvard and Notre Dame have extensive Irish-language courses and degrees. Private-sector foundations, such as Glucksman Ireland House in affiliation with New York University, offer extensive language and culture courses. Online Irish communities and grassroots organizations such as Daltai na gaeilge (www.daltai.org) have also been instrumental in starting a mini diaspora of Irish-language learners all throughout the United States and Canada. Because a language houses not only the stories, songs, and history of a culture but also its quirks—its ways of seeing the world—these efforts seem particularly worthy and vital.

It is also important to understand the essential role that language plays in the story of how the inhabitants of Ireland became the "Celts."

A Little Irish Primer

Hello	*Dhia duit*	*(Jeea dootch or gwitch)*
Goodbye	*Slán*	*(Slawn)*
What is your name?	*Cad is ainm duit?*	*(Cod iss anem dootch?)*
How are you?	*Conas tá tú?*	*(Cawnas taw too?)*
Good enough	*Maith go leor*	*(Maw guh lor)*
To your health	*Sláinte*	*(Slawncha)*
Thank you	*Go raibh maith agat*	*(Gra ma hawgat)*

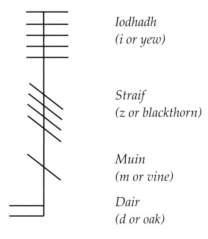

Iodhadh
(i or yew)

Straif
(z or blackthorn)

Muin
(m or vine)

Dair
(d or oak)

Oh My Ogham

Ogham (pronounced *ahum* or *ohm*) is another delightful language conundrum from our ancestral past. One group of scholars holds that it is an ancient druidic hand-signal language, another that it is an ancient Christian language originating around the fourth century and designed to confound Romans, and a third that it is itself a Latinized hieroglyphic. Of a certainty, it is found carved on the edges of standing stones all over Ireland.

Ogham is a series of lines running across and to either side of a central bar. Vertically it is read from bottom to top and horizontally from left to right, with each stick group standing for both a letter and a tree or bush (perhaps a later addition to the letter language). It seems to have been used to name people or places or to count. Originally, it would probably have also been carved onto wooden sticks, none of which still exist.

An ogham stone in a forest in Ireland. Note the incised white sticks along its bottom right side. The sticks may commemorate a person or a date or indicate a direction. Scholars are still not clear on the "Rosetta stone" for ogham.

Language and the Wandering Irish: Did Our Ancient Ancestors Visit Us Before We Were the U.S.?

Picture languages such as ogham and words of Irish origin cropped up in America long before Christopher Columbus made his voyage. In fact, many travelers arrived on these shores well before the great migrations of European invaders.

We know that the Norse came for a visit in the eleventh century A.D., traveling from Greenland and Iceland to the tip of Newfoundland, where they founded an encampment called Vinland at present-day L'Anse aux Meadows, now a Canadian national park. We also

Columcille, a modern megalith park in Bangor, Pennsylvania.

believe that Brendan the Navigator, a sixth-century Irish monk, made a seven-year voyage to the New World in an Irish hide boat called a currach, a voyage that was later duplicated by adventurer Tim Severin (more about that in part 2). These two voyages would be, respectively, 500 and 900 years before the voyage of Christopher Columbus.

But what of our Bronze Age ancestors, the elders from 3000 to 1200 B.C., let's say? For the past twenty years or so, an academic argument has been raging over the speculation that incised stones throughout the Americas could indicate long-ago visitors as diverse as the Chinese, the Phoenicians, the early Norse, and the Iberian Celts (these would be the ancestors of our Milesian Celtic immigrants to Ireland). Stone circles and dolmens from a wide variety of historical periods have been found scattered throughout East Coast locations. Rocks bearing inscriptions that sometimes look like Norse or Phoenician runes and sometimes like the ancient Celtic language of ogham have been discovered in such diverse areas as Massachusetts, Connecticut, and possibly even West Virginia. While most serious scholars debunk these "visitor" stones, a few scholars (backed up by the late Yankton [Sioux] writer and historian Vine Deloria, Jr.) think that the evidence might be worthy of study and that the earlier theory of a single Amerindian migration across the Bering Strait Land Bridge is too narrow for a big world of seafarers and wanderers. Whatever the eventual archeological and anthropological truth of the matter, it is great fun to speculate that great-granddad times hundreds might have been wandering the neighborhood before we lived here.

The Milesians Arrive in Ireland, or, When Did the Irish Become the Celts?

Deep in the green forests of Galicia on the west coast of Spain, a huge and solitary oak tree stands ringed by a thick hedge of prickly blackthorn. A full moon has risen over the sea and it casts its white light across the water in an undulating wedge. Torches glimmer through the forest and reflect on the water below. The men and women who carry them are dressed in long white gowns bordered with knotwork of gold. Around their necks they wear gold lunula, *or hammered crescents. They are druids. Tonight, they are approaching the sacred oak grove for the most important night of prayer in the long history of their tribe. On the morrow, their chief and his family will depart for Inisfail, a small green island far to the north. If it proves hospitable, if they can farm and raise cattle on its emerald hills, their tribe will migrate there. They are the Celts of Galicia in Spain. The year is 500 B.C.*

Is this a true story of the departure of the Spanish Celts for Ireland? If so, is this the first arrival in Ireland of people who self-identify as "Celts"? As with all things anthropological (or Irish), this myth is the source of tremendous controversy. As legends go, it is a huge story—the Milesians arriving in seventy-five great ships, nine of them commanded by the sons of Mil or Milesios, captain of an army that had served the Persian pharaoh of Egypt. The myth would have the entire clan following the path outlined in the map below.

However, archeologists and anthropologists now consider the legend to be variously:

• A huge exaggeration of a small arrival
• A conflation of a number of smaller and more ethnically varied arrivals taking place over hundreds of years, so that Ireland accumulated its Celtic identity over time
• A complete fabrication

From *Song of Ireland* © 2006 by Juilene Osborne-McKnight. Reprinted by permission of Tor / Forge Books. All rights reserved.

Let's begin by examining the myth, as all myths are like popcorn—containing, somewhere, a hard kernel of historical truth. Then we can look at the current archeological and anthropological thinking.

The Arrival of the Milesians
Retold and adapted by Juilene Osborne-McKnight

Fado, fado: long long ago, there lived in Ireland an ancient race of people who never grew sick, never grew old, and never died, for they held power over time. They were known as the Tuatha de Danaan and they had lived on the land for time out of mind.

But from the sea in their great ships came the nine sons of Mil, bearing with them their women and their cattle, their gold and their wine. They landed at the bay on the south tip of the green island and proposed to make war against the Tuatha de Danaan for the rights to the land of Eire.

The Tuatha de Danaan pleaded with the invaders. "Allow us time to prepare, for we do not remember how to make war."

And the Milesians granted their request and retreated to the ninth wave of the sea.

But when they were far out on the water, the Tuatha de Danaan raised a great fog that spread down the hills of Ireland and over the water. The ships were obscured from each other, trapped in a raging wind.

When the wind lifted, five of the nine sons of Mil had been drowned in the sea. The four remaining sons were angry! They chased the Little People of the Tuatha de Danaan all the way to the Plains of Mag Tuiread, where, in a great battle, they defeated the Little People.

Three of the sons of Mil called for the exile of the Tuatha de Danaan. "Banish them from these green hills. For they have cost us our brothers!" they cried.

But the poet Amergin had looked into the eyes of the Little People and he saw that they possessed draoidheacht—*the magic. And he was wise enough to know that if he banished the Little People the magic would go with them.*

So he gave them instead the cities beneath the hollow hills, the rooms beneath the rivers of Eire.

And because they were allowed to remain, the magic remained in Ireland.

Is firinne sin. This is as it is.

So is it indeed? It is useful to unpack current scholarly thinking about just how Ireland came to be known as a "Celtic" country, and to do that we need to look at the wide world of the people known as Celts.

2
The Origins of the Celts

The area outlined in black on the map shows the expansive breadth of the Celtic world before the Roman Empire and particularly before Julius Caesar.

Most people are surprised to discover that the Celts dominated Europe as we now know it, but that is because history is written by the victor. Rome eventually defeated the Celts, who became known in Roman histories, and particularly in the writings of Julius Caesar, as the Gauls. However, those tribal peoples had been in residence in Europe for thousands of years. As a side note, you might be interested to discover that St. Paul's biblical letter to the Galatians is actually written to the large population of Celts living in Turkey! Another interesting fact is that the Celtic tribe known as the Parisii founded the city of Paris around 250 B.C., building a Celtic stronghold in the center of Ile de la Cité, now the site of the cathedral of Notre-Dame de Paris. This was a particularly lucrative site for the ancient Celtic tribe because they charged tolls for people to cross the river!

Those facts aside, scholars are very divided as to the geographic origin point of the Celts. They know, however, that the tribes of Europe spoke a similar language and shared similar cultural, religious, and burial practices.

The earliest and most distinctive Celtic culture is the Urnfield culture of around 1200 B.C., so called because the people burned the ashes of their dead and buried them in urns. Scholars do know that these people lived as far east as what we now call Hungary. The earliest Celtic language (called Proto-Celtic) begins to show up somewhere toward the end of the Urnfield period and the beginning of the Hallstatt period, between 750 and 450 B.C.

The Hallstatt period is a fascinating part of Celtic development. The Celtic tribes of this period mined and controlled the salt mines of what is now the town of Halstatt in the Salzkammergut region of Austria. Salt was a priceless commodity in the ancient world and the Celtic tribes of the region controlled trade and distribution, trading with Greeks and Etruscans. Shafts in one of these mines, which can actually be toured, go to depths of 1,300 feet! A fully preserved Celtic miner was found here in 1734, having been "pickled" by an avalanche sometime around 300 B.C.

Hallstatt Celts scattered throughout Europe and also made and traded linen, mined silver, and developed advanced metalwork skills, creating complex objects in gold and silver. Archeologists have found bronze, amber, and gold goods, funeral wagons, couches, amphorae of wine, and more. The grave of a young Hallstatt Celtic noblewoman discovered at Vix near modern Chatillon-sur-Seine in France was astonishing; she wore a golden crown and amber jewelry, was reclining on a funeral wagon, and was accompanied by silver bowls and cups as well as flagons of wine.

These rich finds indicate a culture that was wealthy, had time for artistic pursuits, traded widely throughout the European and Mediterranean worlds, and had an elite class of ruling families. They also signal a spiritual belief in life after death, as the wagon would serve as transport and the grave goods as food, drink, and status for the newly arrived spirit.

Hallstatt culture was followed by La Tène culture (so named for an archeological site found on Lake Neuchâtel in Switzerland). The La Tène period generally continued from 450 B.C. all the way until Julius Caesar decided to conquer the Gauls in 58 B.C. Generally, this period is characterized by its distinctive art forms of curvilinear animals and repeating braids and knots on bowls, mirrors, cauldrons, and even horse bits, but there was a richness to this culture that included well-constructed and busy *oppida*, or hill cities surrounded by ditched walls. Archeological finds indicate that the Celtic residents of these cities traded with all the major civilizations of the known world and were quite sophisticated.

It is in the space between the Hallstatt and La Tène cultures that archeologists begin to see Celtic artifacts show up in Britain and Ireland. This group of scholars says that the islands became Celtic somewhere between 500 and 200 B.C., an interesting theory as it would match nicely with the tale of the arrival of the Milesians. In fact, the most recent genetic studies done at Oxford show pockets of Viking, Anglo-Saxon, and Norman ancestry in England and a strong link to a migrating group from . . . wait for it . . . Spain in Ireland. The same studies do not show strong links to other Celts of Europe.

Linguists, however, disagree with the La Tène theory because the form of Irish that is spoken in Ireland (Q-Gaelic) is a much earlier form. Thus, they say that Ireland and Britain may very well have been "Celtic" long before the La Tène period, as "Beaker Folk" or "Beaker People" (so called because of the curved beakers they created) moved into the islands with their distinctive form of earlier Gaelic. There is significant evidence of the Beaker form of copper mining and smelting in Ireland as well. Most linguists see the shift from Neolithic to Celtic as a peaceful transition rather than a warrior takeover because, linguistically, language spreads through cooperative community activities rather than warfare. Whatever theory eventually holds water (in a beaker?), we can reasonably draw two conclusions:

1) that Ireland is a Celtic country in language, law, customs, beliefs, and stories and has been for thousands upon thousands of years and

2) that our Milesians of myth may have been just one of many Celtic groups who migrated to Ireland over the long centuries.

Actually, we are lucky that Ireland did indeed become the most Celtic of countries, because, as you will see from the map below, there came a time when the Celtic peoples were almost completely eliminated from the earth. Why? How? The answer to those questions lies in a juggernaut named Julius Caesar.

The Gallic Wars: Julius Caesar vs. the Celts

Long before Julius Caesar came on the scene, there was no love lost between the Romans and the Gauls of Northern Italy and France. The feud went back hundreds of years.

By the time the Roman Empire had finished with its conquest of the world, only the areas outlined in black remained essentially Celtic and Gaelic speaking: Ireland, Scotland above Hadrian's Wall, the Isle of Man, Western Wales and Cornwall, the Brittany coast of France. Although pockets of Celtic practice remained throughout Europe, conquered areas, including France and Britain, became increasingly Romanized.

The Gauls were powerful people and powerful warriors. Men were often close to seven feet tall and loved the art of war. Swinging huge broadswords and shouting the deeds of their ancestors, they often fought naked. Shod in sandals and wearing "battle aprons" to cover their privates, they would protect their bodies with wooden shields as big as doors. Roman historians tell of them bearing down on their enemies undressed but for helmets with articulating birdwings— naked and fearsome, flying and screaming.

Women were also among the warriors, fighting side by side with their men, as Celtic society did not differentiate the genders by sexist standards. Women were considered equal to men in intelligence and prowess and under the law as well. Roman historian Ammianus Marcellinus (330-395 A.D.) says of Celtic women warriors, "A whole band of foreigners will be unable to cope with one [Gaul] in a fight, if he calls in his wife, stronger than he by far and with flashing eyes; least of all when she swells her neck and gnashes her teeth, and poising her huge white arms, begins to rain blows mingled with kicks, like shots discharged by the twisted cords of a catapult."

The Romans had already mythologized the Celts, and Rome had a long, long memory. Some five centuries before Julius Caesar, Gauls had moved into the Po Valley of Italy (now the area near Mantua, of Shakespearean fame). These Celts were tribal and warlike and imposed themselves upon the resident Etruscans. One tribe called the Senones, under chief Brennus, attacked the city of Clusium. The Etruscans asked Rome for help and in the resulting skirmishes, the Senones lost some men and went rampaging toward Rome, defeating the defending Roman army, laying siege to and pillaging the city, and forcing the Romans to hole up on the Capitoline Hill for nearly a year. Eventually, to get rid of Brennus and his warriors, the Romans agreed to pay the Gauls a hefty fee of 1,000 pounds (the weight, not the currency) of gold.

Even while the Romans were paying, they were complaining. The historian Livy tells us, "Insult was added to what was already sufficiently disgraceful, for the weights which the Gauls brought for weighing the metal were heavier than standard, and when the Roman commander objected the insolent barbarian flung his sword into the scale, saying, "Woe to the vanquished!" (*Vae victus* in Latin— considered by many scholars to be the best retort in all history.)

This incident insulted the Romans and stayed in their memories

The Dying Gaul, a marble statue in the Capitoline Museum in Rome. The Gaul is tall, in naked fighting form, wearing his golden torc (collar) and his hair limed back for battle. He rests upon his large shield and has cast his broadsword aside. Blood trickles from a wound in his side and his face is in agony, as his wound is mortal. It is likely that this statue is a Roman marble copy of a Greek bronze from around the second century A.D.

and in their histories for hundreds of years; Julius Caesar used that xenophobia to his advantage.

Julius Caesar had personal reasons for wanting to start a war with his Gallic neighbors over the Alps. For one thing, he was deeply in debt and needed to fill up his coffers. For another, in alliance with Pompey and Crassus, Caesar had aspirations toward ruling Rome. Through political machinations, he managed to get himself named proconsul for both Cisalpine and Transalpine Gaul (Gallic Italy below the Alps and Gaul above the Alps). Thus, he positioned himself perfectly for what he wanted to achieve.

Next, he found the ideal excuse for starting a war. The Helvetii tribe, who had been living in Switzerland, were being crowded out and decided to migrate into the heart of Gaul (modern-day France). Tribes of Celts who had become very Romanized feared the warlike Helvetii and petitioned Rome for help. Caesar had his excuse. He defeated the Helvetii and forced them to return to Switzerland. After that first encounter, Caesar justified the need to conquer all of Gaul and from 58 B.C. to 52 B.C. did just that, commenting on the process throughout in his lengthy field report *Commentaries on the Gallic War.* (If you have never read it, it is a fascinating study of the justifications for imperialism and xenophobia while also serving as a brilliant military tactical manual.)

In some ways throughout the process, the Gallic Celts were their own worst enemy. Many of them, particularly in the tribes surrounding the Alps, had become quite Romanized, trading with Rome for wine and cloth, wearing Roman clothes, and often speaking Latin. These Romanized tribes waffled back and forth throughout the wars, sometimes swinging their allegiance toward their ancestral Celtic identity, but at others craving protection from Caesar or declaring their allegiance to Rome.

Celtic society functioned as a series of small towns, each of which gave allegiance to one chief. While these Gallic groups might trade, feast, or intermarry with each other, they might also steal horses or go to war. Throughout their history, they had never managed to unite themselves into a single, cohesive cultural group.

To defeat Caesar, that cohesion became necessary, and there arose in their midst a stunning leader who came within inches of driving Caesar out of Gaul. His name was Vercingetorix, a young chieftain of the Arveni tribe of Southwest France (near present-day Auvergne). Nearly seven feet tall, he wielded a broadsword taller than many people, but his true skills were intelligence and oratory. Tribe by tribe, Vercingetorix convinced the insular and bristly Celts of Gaul that unless they could band together and defeat Julius Caesar, the Celtic way of life was at an end. He could not have been more prophetic.

The Celts were legendary horsemen; in his youth, Vercingetorix had served in a Roman cavalry unit. He knew how the Roman army was organized and how it fought. He managed to defeat the Roman army in the battle of Gergovia, killing nearly fifty Centurions and more than seven hundred legionaries.

He also understood that the massive Roman army moved on its stomach. Once he had united the tribes, he instituted a scorched-earth policy, burning towns, stores, fields of wheat—anything that could allow the Roman army to eat. Unfortunately, his tribesmen wanted one great *oppidum* left extant: Avaricum, near modern Bourges. Caesar captured it, utilized the supplies, slaughtered most of the inhabitants, and chased Vercingetorix and his army all the way to the *oppidum* at Alesia (modern-day Alise-Sainte-Reine, near Dijon).

Here Caesar trapped the army on the hill by building a huge siege wall called a circumvallation. In order to prevent reinforcements from reaching Vercingetorix, Caesar then built a contravallation—a siege wall around the siege wall. No one could get in and no one could get out. Eventually Vercingetorix was forced to surrender; historian Plutarch says that the chieftain rode up in full armor on a white horse, cast down his sword, and sat at Caesar's feet.

Vercingetorix Surrenders to Caesar, by French painter Lionel Noel Royer, 1899. The original hangs in the Crozatier Museum in France. (Image used here by licensing arrangement with Art Resource Fine Art Licensing, New York, USA)

The fate of Vercingetorix was as horrible as the fate of all Gaul. Caesar threw this free and wild warrior Celt into a Roman prison, where he held him for almost six years. Then, in Caesar's triumphal parade, he marched Vercingetorix through the streets in an oxen yoke, with a sign saying *Behold the Gaul,* after which Vercingetorix was slaughtered.

The Gauls of France fared no better. By the time Caesar's war was over, a million Gauls had been slaughtered and a million sold into slavery. France was no longer the stronghold of Celtic culture in the world, and the islands of Britain/Scotland/Wales and Ireland were left to preserve the ancient Celtic ways. It is fair to assume that Gauls who could escape did so; a pocket of the Gaelic language still exists on the Brittany coast of France, and the Veneti tribe, who were master sailors, may well have sailed for Britain or ferried tribal escapees to the safer shore, but we simply do not know.

Britain would later fall to the same Roman fate. Caesar had attempted an invasion of Britain in 55 and 54 B.C. but both times the weather was awful, his ships were blown out to sea or dashed on the rocks, and food was in short supply, so he abandoned the plan. However, nearly a hundred years later, the emperor Claudius began the long campaign to subdue and Romanize Britain, and although the great queen Boudicca led a valiant and nearly successful rebellion, the Romans eventually destroyed the druid center of Mona in 60 A.D. and effectively took Britain from a Celtic country to a Roman conquest.

Thus, the Celtic world shrank to a thread of its former glory—tiny pockets in Brittany, above Hadrian's Wall in Scotland, and Ireland ("Hibernia" to the Romans). Although Ireland is clearly visible across the water from Britain and although there is plenty of archeological evidence in Ireland of Roman trade, the Romans never invaded Ireland. Had that not been so, all indications of the great Celtic tribes who dominated Europe for so long might have vanished completely, a civilization with little record and no cultural memory. This makes Ireland a treasure trove, for much of what we know of the Celts— their appearance, lifestyle, beliefs, social and cultural customs—we know because Ireland was not conquered by Rome.

3

Life in Ancient Ireland

In 1903 in Somerset, England, archeologists found a murdered caveman estimated to date back to 7000 B.C. As if this were not astonishing enough, in 1996 scientists extracted one of his molars and compared his DNA to that of residents in the nearby village of Cheddar. Of twenty people tested, they found two who were related to the ancient skeleton. One of them, a schoolteacher named Targett, was a direct descendant of the caveman.

If you are Irish-American, this story could very well be yours. Some bog-man or buried warrior, some queen or wandering druid, was your ancestor. You carry their stories in your very bones.

So when we study how they lived, what they believed, even what they ate and drank, we are, in effect, returning to our own roots, sitting down at the "family table," 2,000 years ago.

You might be surprised to learn that our ancestors were sophisticated and spiritual, warlike and loquacious, bound to strict codes of honor, and in love with the spoken word, holding stories in such high reverence that even battles would stop immediately if a poet so ordered.

Let's begin by looking at the ordinary, everyday details of life in ancient Ireland.

Ancient Irish life was tribal and centered in the village. Small clan groups lived in *raths* or ring forts that consisted of circular huts with a thatched roof. At the center of each village would be a larger hut for the chief of the group. Chieftains were elected based upon their ability to govern wisely and to protect and provide for the clan.

Ring forts were often surrounded by two to three ditches, some lined with stones or sticks, depending upon the tribe's wealth. A causeway might lead to the main gate.

The author performing a storytelling in the Grianan Ailigh ring fort in Northern Ireland. Photo by Diana Florence Koch.

The clan's economy was largely based on cattle; the ancient Irish *boaire* or cattleman was a respected position. A man's wealth was reckoned by the number of cattle he possessed. Cattle were the source of meat, milk, and leather for clothing, and they were guarded, bred carefully, and even purified in special rituals. They would be pastured in the fields outside the rath during the day and herded into pens or even into the rath itself at night. Some raths might have been as small as a single farm, others could have housed 200 inhabitants, but more than 50,000 ring forts existed throughout Ireland.

Another interesting dwelling place for our ancient ancestors was the crannog—a manmade island in a lake or bog that could only be reached by a single causeway. Obviously, this was a good defensive position, but the construction of crannogs shows tremendous ingenuity. Upright logs were driven into the bottom of a shallow lake and then a firm base was created with peat, soil, or gravel. Then a dwelling or even a little village of two to three dwellings were built upon the base. More than a thousand of these have been discovered in Ireland and Scotland.

Ancient Irish Social Classes

As with any other society, society in ancient Ireland consisted of classes, listed below in descending order. We will discuss each of these categories as we move into the stories of ancient Ireland, but it is interesting to note the levels of society that were open to women. Unlike the Romans or later medieval societies dominated by men, ancient Irish society was remarkably nonsexist. It also valued knowledge and its dispersal above almost any other activity.

- *Ard Ri*, or high king (for example, Conchobar Mac Nessa in Ulster or Cormac Mac Art at Tara)—more about these worthies later.
- Chieftains. Ireland was a clan-based, rath-based society and each clan and rath elected its own chief, based on his physical fitness to fight and his wisdom to dispense law and justice with an even hand. Some of these chiefs were women, such as Medb of Connacht, whose story you will read later. As a side note, you might be interested to know that the real, historical Macbeth did not steal his kingship or have it conferred upon him but was elected to his post by the ancient Celtic system of *tanaistre*, i.e., the voted election of a successor.

- Druids. We will discuss druids extensively in part 2, but they were the professoriate and priests of ancient Ireland. A druid trained for twenty years to accrue the knowledge required to serve and teach his or her people. Both men and women could be druids and it was possible that there were levels of druids in ancient Ireland. The person of a druid was so sacred in ancient Ireland that to harm him resulted in a sentence of instant death. The knowledge of druids was never written down; in fact, doing so was forbidden by law. Knowledge is power and druids were an initiate group with tremendous power.
- Warriors. Not only did Ireland require protection from outside invaders, but tribes often went to war with each other. Warriors were highly skilled and trained in the martial arts and had to pass rigorous testing to be accepted into the elite groups—the Red Branch before 100 A.D. and the Fenians in the third century A.D. We will talk further of these warrior societies as well. Women could also become warriors in ancient Ireland. Warriors were the very elite noblemen and women of ancient Ireland.
- The *aos dána*, or people of the arts. These were the learned folks of Ireland and they had the privilege of free passage on any of Ireland's roads and the offer of hospitality in any village, that hospitality being both sacred and mandated by law. The aos dána were poets, bards, storytellers, and genealogists and again their training was extensive—a dozen years at least, by most historical accounts. A master of these arts was known by the term *ollamh*. The literal English translation of that word today would be "professor." Again both men and women could join these ranks. *Brehons,* or lawyers, were also members of the aos dana. At one time in Ireland there were more than 1,200 lawyers! Ancient Irish law was specific, extensive, and protected every level of society, even the lowest. Interestingly, an association named Aosdána was created in Ireland in the 1980s and consists of 250 living artists throughout Ireland. Membership is a singular honor and affords the writer, artist, architect, or dancer the same kind of elite status given to bards and storytellers in ancient Ireland.
- *Boaire.* These cattlemen were much respected by the aristocracy and heavily protected under the law.
- Freemen. Although not landowners, they were protected under the law and had the right to vote. These freemen could be further subdivided:

- Craftsmen, such as blacksmiths and metalworkers. Metalwork was elaborate and prized as both jewelry and the accoutrements of war, such as broadswords and iron bands for chariot wheels.
- Farmers, laborers, and tradesmen.
- Bondsmen/women. These could be captives, strangers with no clan affiliations, or even criminals. They were slaves, but Irish society still recognized slaves as human beings, so bondspeople could be emancipated or even made full members of the tribe if their behavior and service while in bondage earned the respect of the tribe.

Above and below all of these classes in Irish society was the clan—the extended network of relations who formed your tribe.

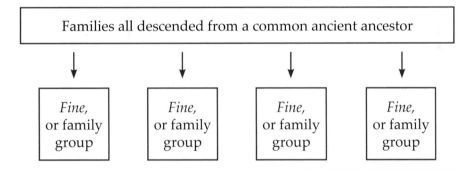

All *fines* (pronounced *fee-nahs*) further subdivided into clan relationships based on closeness of relationship to the clan chieftain.

- *Gel-fine*
- *Derbh-fine*
- *Lar-fine*
- *Inn-fine*

To simplify, think of this as brothers/first cousins/cousins once removed/second cousins, etc. The relationship system of ancient Ireland and Scotland was so complex that it boggles the modern mind.

Marriage and Family Life in Ancient Ireland

Ancient Irish history is filled with great love stories. Some are funny, others tragic, but they all have in common the ancient Irish sense of love as an essential life force.

Marriage customs in ancient Ireland were rather complicated. For example, in Fenian times, at a warrior feast, a warrior who had distinguished himself in battle could stand up and claim any woman as his bride. However, this does not mean that women were powerless in the choice of bridegroom. Ancient Irish stories often tell us of feasts in which a woman could approach a man with a cup of marriage in hand. If he accepted and drank from the goblet she offered, they were, in effect, betrothed. Some of these cups must have been declined as well, and it's terrible, even from this distance, to imagine the young woman's complete embarrassment and heartbreak.

Of course, parents and high-ranking members of society such as chieftains could also arrange marriages and determine dowries.

Marriage contracts were elaborate and had many different levels, but both men and women were protected under Irish law. If they divorced, they left the marriage with the same property they started with. Ancient Irish law did not favor either gender.

Trial marriages were also common; couples could be handfasted (literally their wrists tied together, which may be where we get the term "tying the knot"). They might then enter a trial marriage of a year and a day. If it did not work out, divorce was completely no fault. Handfasting has become quite popular in modern weddings and is also the preferred ceremony nowadays in pagan and wiccan weddings.

Some men in ancient Irish societies were allowed to have more than one wife, provided they could afford to do so, as the law provided for every child birthed and did not differentiate between "legitimate" and "illegitimate" children. Interestingly, a first wife, or *cet muintir*, whose husband decided to take more than one wife had very strict rights under Irish law. First, she had the right to be consulted, and if she did not approve of the additional choices, she had the right of veto. Other wives or women were also classified before the law, all the way down to "love woman."

Once the second or third wife came into the home, the first wife had some rather harsh rights as well. She could, for example, beat or torment (really do any kind of damage short of death) the wife for the first three days of the new marriage, after which she had to accept her and get along. By and large, these arrangements seem to have been tolerated well. Perhaps for women whose men were often hunting or making war, the companionship and a helpmeet or two overrode other considerations, or perhaps in a culture that was very matter of fact about sexuality, such arrangements were not a cause for jealousy.

Whatever the reasons, we do know that men with multiple wives were often the more powerful and therefore the wealthier of Celtic society, because the property rights and divorce rights of all the women in the arrangement were specified and protected.

We do not have accounts of women taking more than one husband, but we do have some of very libidinous women such as Medb of Connacht, who were admired and not censured in the ancient literature.

Children were especially prized in ancient Celtic society. Not only was there no stigma attached to births outside of marriage, but children were carefully trained in both knowledge and proper behaviors. In the third century, for example, we are told that King Cormac Mac Art maintained a huge school on the Hill of Tara. Called the *Teach Forradh* (pronounced *Chalk Forodd*), this school educated young people in history, math, genealogy, philosophy, and mythology as well as martial arts. Their teachers were both druids and warriors.

Warriors in that same period abided by a very strict code regarding children. Among other laws, if a warrior managed to orphan a child during war, he was responsible for finding a good home for that child.

Children in Irish society were often fostered out, at around age seven or even younger. Girls would stay in fosterage until fourteen, boys until seventeen, the ages at which marriage usually took place. Children of the upper classes lived with aunts or uncles or cousins, sometimes in nearby villages not their own. These related foster parents were responsible for feeding and clothing the children but also for making sure that they were educated and brought up to abide by the proper laws and customs of Irish society. Such arrangements would have linked villages and family groups together, and we can speculate that it might have allowed young people to meet marriage prospects in other villages who were not so closely related as those in the immediate clan. The brehon laws specifying the responsibilities of foster parents make the worth of children obvious. Many Irish stories show the relationships of the foster parents and children as being even closer than those of the biological parents and children, which makes sense considering that the children spent their most formative years in fosterage.

The Men that God Made Mad: Feasting, Fighting, and Telling Tales

British writer G. K. Chesterton penned a famous little poem about the Irish:

> The great Gaels of Ireland
> are the men that God made mad,
> for all their wars are merry
> and all their songs are sad.

Chesterton is not far off when he talks about our ancient ancestors. War was a dance, a spectacle, an event worthy of the tallest of tales. The *Táin bó Cúailnge*, Ireland's epic war poem, spends much time telling us—in loving detail worthy of a red-carpet occasion—what the combatants are wearing, right down to their belts, their sandals, and the colors woven into their cloaks and tunics.

In ancient Ireland, war was often conducted in neighboring counties. While you might argue with your clan, you generally took your wars outside your clan borders. These skirmishes could be about land, cattle raids, women, or all of the above at once.

Irish warriors must have made an impressive sight as they approached on the battlefield. They were tall. Many rode magnificent horses and the very best of them were driven to battle in wickerwork chariots, by charioteers who are celebrated in the literature of war. For example, the great hero Cú Chulainn had a cherished driver named Laeg Mac Riangabra.

Irish battle attire was spectacular to the point of narcissism. The warriors' hair was coiffed and often limed, their long bushy mustaches drooping past their chins. They wore plaid *braichs* (from which we get the term "britches"), a kind of ancient set of Capri pants that came to just below the knee. (For those golfers among us, the late Payne Stewart wore these as his regular golf costume.) They wore huge plaid cloaks but of a different plaid from the braichs. These cloaks were held at the shoulder by penannular brooches. Tunics were often embroidered with scenes of hounds or deer or twining birds, and a thick leather belt at the waist could hold knives or daggers. A huge broadsword hung down the center of the warrior's back and the ensemble was completed with a boss, or shield, also heavily decorated. It was important that these warriors be in excellent physical shape; fines were levied against a warrior who gained weight.

Two great warrior societies arose in Ireland. Although we do not know where the line between exaggeration and history can be drawn in the stories of these two armies, they form the basis for hundreds of tales of heroes, battles, and loves lost and found. They were:

- The Red Branch, the army of Ulster under King Conchobar Mac Nessa. From the ranks of this standing army came Cú Chulainn, the greatest single warrior of Irish mythology and the hero of the epic *Táin bó Cúailnge* (more on him and on the *Táin* later).
- The Fenians, the army of Ireland under the great leader Fionn Mac Cumhail. This army defended Ireland throughout the reign of King Cormac Mac Art in the third century.

Both armies lived by a strict code of behavior, and again, both included female members, although the preponderance of warriors were men. Their culture included tales of great deeds, with warriors vying for the best haunch of deer or boar at massive feasts by embellishing stories of their own prowess. The best of those stories were often immortalized by bards (who sang of them with a small, portable harp called a *clarsach*) or storytellers (called *seanchai*, pronounced *shan-a-key*) who would take the stories from rath to rath, sometimes embroidering them even as they traveled. Thus did history become myth.

Of course, this storytelling was always accompanied by eating and drinking on a Herculean scale. Ancient Ireland was a foodie's dream; while we sometimes think of ancient societies as eating nothing but gruel and cooked venison, nothing could be further from the truth, as you will see from the chart below.

Meats	Fish	Grains	Dairy	Vegetables and Fruits	Beverages	Condiments
Venison	Salmon	Stirabout (porridge)	Milk (both cow and goat)	Leeks	Beer	Honey
Boar	Cod	Wheat bread	Buttermilk	Cabbage	Honey mead	Salt
Mutton		Barley bread	Curds and whey	Parsnips	Wine (imported)	Garlic
Beef			Butter	Turnips	Water	
Goat				Apples		
				Pears		

Honey was so important in ancient Ireland that an entire section of the brehon law is devoted to bees, beekeeping, and honey. Honey was eaten in cones and used to sweeten milk, to make honey-cakes, as a dip for fish or meat, and to make honey mead, the potent alcoholic drink of ancient Ireland. It was the liquid gold of our ancestors.

Meats were also cooked and seasoned in a variety of ways, but the tenderest were often cooked in a *fulacht fiadh* like the one pictured opposite. Hundreds of these have been found scattered throughout Ireland. The pit would be dug and filled with water, which would be kept hot, or even boiling, by the addition of fire-heated stones. This long process would cause the meat to be so tender that it would fall off the bone. The haunch, considered the best delicacy, was given to the king, the highest-ranking warrior or visitor, or the one who told the best story!

Fish, of course, were a staple of the ancient Irish diet; in 2014, archeologists found a fish trap in a Dublin quay that may date all the way back to the time of the builders of the ancient Irish court tombs such as Newgrange! Salmon in particular had sacred or wisdom connotations, which we will see in our discussion of the Fenians.

Mead was considered an Irish delicacy—a drink brewed of fermented honey and spices such as cinnamon and cloves. It was often given to guests upon arrival, a custom that is continued in Ireland at the Feast at Bunratty Castle, a touristy medieval event in a Norman keep that nonetheless greets guests with little cups of delicious honey mead.

A *fulacht fiadh,* or meat-steaming pit.

Note, however, the absence of potatoes in any of this discussion. Potatoes (which probably originated with the Incas of ancient Peru) were not introduced to Ireland until the sixteenth century.

The Brehon Laws

Thus far, we have mentioned the brehon laws in the context of beekeeping, fosterage, marriage, and social classes, but every Irish-American should be familiar with these laws, because they go a long way toward explaining our immersion in the professions of law and policing as well as our deep and abiding sense of social justice and fairness (see sidebar of brehon laws). The term *brehon* derives from the ancient Irish word *breitheamh,* which means "judge," but it is likely that our Gaelic ancestors called this body of laws the *Féineachas,* which, loosely translated, means "law of the free farmers." The laws are actually deeply rooted in the ancient clan system of Ireland. The ancient Irish designed the laws, lived by the laws, adjudicated cases under the laws, and, in general, were so obsessed with the laws that although what has been translated thus far constitutes five huge volumes, scholars estimate that more than three times that amount still exists untranslated!

You will see the laws referred to as medieval, but that is incorrect. Although monks began to write the laws down on vellum in the seventh or eighth century A.D., Irish law had existed in oral form for hundreds and perhaps thousands of years prior to the coming of Christianity to Ireland. However, writing in ancient Ireland, as we discussed in our brief look at the druids, was forbidden. Lawyers and judges had to memorize not only all of the laws but all of the precedent cases related to any specific field and had to render opinions and interpretations on case law and reparations from this vast storehouse of memory! Neither lawyers nor judges ruled on the law; they interpreted and gave opinions for the chief, who ruled.

At one point during the reign of Conchobar Mac Nessa in Ulster there were too many lawyers—more than 1,200 by some estimates—with some simply declaring themselves lawyers with no training. Also, ancient texts say that the lawyers spoke in some kind of arcane, unintelligible language. The result was that a system of training was introduced. Young people who wished to interpret the law now studied and memorized (sometimes for decades) and then took a standing oral exam before a panel of brehons.

Of course, as with all Irish professions, many women were lawyers and judges, and we actually do possess their written rulings and opinions from medieval times on a number of subjects. For the very best look at the role of women of law in ancient Ireland, it is important (and delightful) to read Peter Tremayne's (the pseudonym for Celtic scholar Peter Berresford Ellis) Sister Fidelma series of law mysteries.

The first three tomes of the ancient law tracts are known as the *Seanchus Mor*, literally translated as the *Big Record* but probably referred to as the *Great Law* or *Great Code*. According to many sources, one of the first persons to ever write the law down was King Cormac Mac Art, during the third century. Although there are no extant copies of his *Psalter of Tara*, his *Book of Acaill,* a compendium of criminal laws, has been translated.

Some Unusual and Interesting Brehon Laws

- The fine for breaking the nail of a harpist is four cows.
- Landowners surrounding a beekeeper's farm are entitled to a portion of honey, as the bees gather from their flowers.
- A first wife is entitled to the dowry of a second wife
- A man who does not give a pregnant woman the food she craves must pay a fine.
- Murder is compensated by an honor price or *eric*.
- A "handfasted" couple is allowed a trial marriage of one year; the date for walking away is February first. However, if they get pregnant or bear a child during that year, they are married by law and neither can walk away.
- The insane should not marry or bear children.
- Hospitality, even to strangers, is the law. Kings appoint a *brughaid*, who keeps an inn at which everyone is given beer, bread, butter, and a good bed, at no cost. Individual homes are also required to offer hospitality.

These laws were often interpreted at *feisanna,* or festivals. Such festivals were held throughout Ireland, in the same way that county fairs are often held in the United States. However, cases were brought before the law at these festivals because the aos dána (remember that these folks were the learned class of Ireland, which included poets, bards, and lawyers) would be present and could hear them. Four great festivals were held in Ireland every year (see below) and suits were adjudicated at these times.

The brehon laws of Ireland were crushed by Queen Elizabeth I, who invaded Ireland (more about this in part 3) and imposed British rule upon its people.

The Great Irish Festivals, or Feisanna

Imbolc: February 1-7. Imbolc celebrated the midpoint between winter solstice and spring equinox. For this reason, it was considered the beginning of spring. The name derives from the Irish *i mbolg* (literally "in the hold or belly"), which refers to pregnant ewes who gave birth to lambs in early spring. Because lambs are the origin of the holiday, it was dedicated to Brighid/Anu/Dana, a three-faceted goddess and protector of everything creative. The primary figure of the trinity was Brighid; she protected ewes, hearth fires, poetry, black-smiths, pregnant women, and midwives. In ancient times, it was be-lieved that she would visit and bless the hearths of the people, leaving her footprints in the ashes. Because Imbolc signified spring and a return to light, the festival utilized candles and hearth fires as symbols of hope. It may be that the festival predated the Celts because passage graves such as the Mound of the Hostages on the Hill of Tara, which dates to before 3000 B.C. and in which archeologists have found the remains and grave goods of more than 250 people, is aligned with the sun on Imbolc.

Eventually, when Christianity came to Ireland, the festival became known as St. Brigid's Day and most scholars believe that St. Brigid is a Christianization of the ancient Celtic goddess. St. Brigid is a beloved Irish figure; you will still see St. Brigid's crosses above doors and even in Irish shops. The "cross," which is woven of reeds, is the symbol of the sun and therefore of Imbolc. Many Irish legends refer to St. Brigid as the midwife of Christ, thus hearkening back again to the ancient goddess and her protection of midwives. It is also interesting to note that Candlemas, the Christian festival in which candles are blessed, takes place on February 2. In part 2, we will take a more in-depth look at the way pre-Christian practices blended into the Christian practices of our Irish ancestors.

Beltaine: May 1. You will see this holiday referred to as *Beltane,* but the Irish spelling was *Beltaine,* pronounced *Belltawnya.* This was a festival characterized by fire. Belenos was an ancient Irish deity of fire and the sun, symbolized by a chariot and a great spoked wheel. However, scholars are not sure that the festival of Beltaine was named after this particular god. What they do know is that this was a fertility festival, celebrated in Ireland with important fire rituals, flowers, and greenery.

One of the important functions of this day was the purification of cattle. Because cattle were the basis of the Irish economy, ensuring their health and fertility was paramount. On Beltaine two great fires would be built on the top of a hill, and cattle would be driven through the smoke as a ritual of purification. When the fires had died down to a reasonable level, humans would jump over them as well, often to symbolize passage to a new relationship or, for pregnant women, safe birth for the baby. Of course, because it was May, the festival was also celebrated with woven garlands of flowers, green boughs above doorways, and coupling, the act of fertility itself.

Lughnasa: August 1. You have probably already guessed that this was a festival to celebrate the first harvest, but did you know that it was named after our man/god Lugh Lamfhada (long spear arm)? The Son of the Light was preeminent throughout the Celtic world. (Ancient Lugdunum became Lyon, France, and many scholars believe that London is also named for Lugh.) Lugh was able to do all things well. He could forge at a smithy and ride a great horse, hold his breath under water for hours, fight without ever becoming exhausted, and throw his spear with perfect precision. He was also a harper, poet, wheelwright, healer, and genealogist, and that's not all! Lugh managed to defeat the evil giant Balor of the One Eye, who could kill everyone in his range of vision simply by opening his eyelid and looking at them. Lugh whirled his sling over his head and put out Balor's eye.

Supposedly, it was Lugh who instituted the thanksgiving feast for the first harvest, which involved climbing to the tops of mountains to present the first corn to the creator. He also introduced the Tailteann Games, in memory of his foster mother. These games took place during the last two weeks in July. (The Irish reckoned time by nights and by the waxing and waning of the moon. So two weeks of nights, or fourteen nights, became known as a fortnight.) The games began with druids singing funeral songs in memory of the dead and then morphed into horseraces, chariot races, footraces, swimming races, fights—an ancient Iron Man competition! Dancing, singing, story-telling, and great readings of the law were also featured. The games concluded with Lughnasa. These celebrations supposedly took place near the modern area of Telltown (*Tailtin*), in County Meath (the county shown in the photo here).

Interestingly, one holdover from this ancient festival is the climbing of mountains in pilgrimage. For example, pilgrims still scale Croagh Patrick in County Mayo on the last Sunday in July. Many climb barefoot!

Samhain: October 31-November 1. Samhain (pronounced *Sow-win*) is the granddaddy of all Celtic festivals because it is "the time between the times." The days grow shorter and turn toward darkness, and our ancient ancestors believed that as that happened, the veil that separated this world from the world of the Others (An Sidhe) grew thin. On this night, of all nights, our ancestors believed that the souls of the dead could return and the Little People could come through the doorway. The Little People, as we have discussed earlier, could be . . . unpredictable. Among their number were those who cared for human beings, married them, dealt fairly with them. But there were equally as many who might try to kill humans, steal their children and replace them with changeling babies, or trick them into the world of the Sidhe, in which

time did not pass the same way it passes on earth. A human tricked into the world of the Sidhe might believe that he had been among them for three days, only to return to earth to discover that 300 years had passed and everyone he knew was long dead. For that reason, Samhain was a dangerous time in the Celtic mind and numerous rituals evolved as protection. Our ancestors might have left out food and drink as a gift for the Others or worn masks to frighten them away. Skulls with candles in them might have been hung in trees either to invite the spirits of the dead or to scare off the Sidhe.

Because Samhain also marked the turning of the year toward darkness, fire was a big part of the ritual. Some accounts say that all fires were extinguished on this night and a great bonfire was lighted. Runners then carried torches from hill to hill and fires blossomed on all the hilltops as a ritual way to keep the darkness at bay. Pagans and wiccans have adopted all of these holidays as "Sabbats" but the original intent of these festivals was to acknowledge the turning points between solstices and equinoxes. Our ancestors were very much aware of seasonal changes and movements of the lights and planets and marked all of those turning points with festivals.

Eventually, of course, Samhain permuted into Halloween and All Saints Day.

Irish Ancestral Customs in America

Halloween costumes derive directly from our Celtic ancestors: to scare away the Others who might come through the door, wear a scarier mask!

The lighting of pumpkins also has a long Celtic history, first in hanging lighted skulls in the Samhain trees. Our ancestors believed that the soul resides in the head. The person who owned many heads was well protected by the spirits who once inhabited those heads. Later, the Irish and the English carved faces into turnips on Samhain, now turned Halloween.

Our ancient ancestors used to bob for apples on Halloween! The patterns of their teeth marks in the apple might predict that they would find their true love in the upcoming year.

A custom not necessarily related to Halloween is nonetheless Celtic in origin. In order to ward off bad luck, Americans will say "knock wood." This derives from an ancient druidic ritual. Druid sacred ceremonies were held in oak groves in which a great oak was the center of a ritual circle. Druids believed that a tree has its arms raised in a constant state of prayer, so they would knock three times on the trunk with a ritual dagger to call up those protective spirits.

4

The Four Cycles of Storytelling

Thus far, we have mentioned Ireland as a storytelling culture and you have read the myth of the coming of the Milesians. However, it is most important to note that storytelling was not a side dish to the Irish; it was the main course at the feast! If you grew up in an Irish-American family, it is likely that you already know this fact— Grandma who told you stories of the banshee, Uncle Frank who stood up at every family occasion and sang old ballads, Aunt Mame who whispered tales about the black sheep in the family.

To the ancient Irish, these tellers were revered and precious. The name for a traditional Irish storyteller is *seanchai*. A seanchai was a high-ranking member of the aos dána, the learned people of Ireland whom we have mentioned before and who had the freedom of the Irish roads. When a seanchai wandered into a village with his retinue, people vied for the chance to host him and feed him. Entire villages would gather to hear the seanchai's tales. Not only did he bring with him the tales of the Little People and of the great heroes and love stories of Ireland, but he also brought the news of the day—what was happening in all of the other distant raths of Ireland.

For thousands of years, these stories were passed down orally and never written down. An elder seanchai would train the younger aspirants, not only in the stories themselves but how to tell them— how to captivate audiences gathered about them in the firelight.

Eventually, when Christianity came to Ireland, the monks began to take down these old stories in the scriptoria of the monastery, part of their sacred duty to preserve learning. Sometimes they changed the particularly pagan ones, giving them a suspiciously Christian spin in an anachronistic time period, but we owe these monks a tremendous debt of gratitude. There are literally thousands of stories in the Four Cycles that we are about to discuss. Without the monks, all of them would have been lost to us.

Estimates are that there are thousands of these vellum stories, some collected, some curated, many not, some functioning as books, and still others as vellum pages. In order to classify what we do have and give it some form and sense, scholars have divided these stories into four main categories or cycles:

- **The Mythological Cycle**. These are the stories of the ancient races of Ireland and the Little People, the Tuatha de Danaan.
- **The Ulster Cycle**. This cycle offers the stories of the Red Branch of Ulster, King Conchobar Mac Nessa, and particularly the great epic poem of ancient Ireland, the *Táin bó Cúailnge* (*Cattle Raid of Cooley*). This set of stories takes place roughly in the late part of the first century B.C.
- **The Fenian Cycle**. These are the stories of Fionn Mac Cumhail (pronounced *Finn Mac Cool*), leader of the Fenian warriors of Ireland in the second and third century A.D.
- **The Cycle of Kings**. Think of this as a "thread" cycle. The stories here are of the great kings of Ireland. They start in prehistory and run all the way up to Brian Boru and the Battle of Clontarf in 1014 A.D. Because Cormac Mac Art is included among them, we will conflate the Fenian and Kings cycles.

A Storytelling

In order to understand the importance of these stories to our ancestors, we will contextualize each of these cycles and look at a story from each.

The Mythological Cycle

We could say that these are the stories of prehistory. It is a bit snobbish of us to say that (it wasn't prehistory to the people who lived it), but it was indeed prewritten history. We have already mentioned Balor of the One Eye, Nuada, and Lugh Lamfhada, but this cycle is replete with tales of gods and goddesses, great loves and lost loves, and times when the lives of the Others intersected with the lives of humans. Think of myth as a piece of popcorn. Inside the salty, puffy, and buttery treat, you will sometimes encounter the hard kernel. Myth has grown aroundthe kernel and gathered "spices," if you will, by being exaggerated and passed along from teller to teller (think of that party game "Whisper Down the Lane"). However, inside any myth are kernels of real history as well as knowledge about the people of the age. When the myths are written down, the time of the writers is superimposed upon them. Below is one such tale, in which the lives of the magical Others become entwined with the lives of human beings.

The Wooing of Etain
Retold and adapted by Juilene Osborne-McKnight

Long ago or longer, on the island known as Eire-of-the-Sea, there lived a magical race of people called the Sidhe. The Sidhe were special folk who never grew old or sick or sad and who never died.

Midir, the king of these fairy folk, was rotund and red-bearded, full of laughter. The greatest joy of Midir's life was his wife, Etain, the fairy queen. Etain was kind and beautiful. Her hair was the color of the copper leaves of autumn, her skin as white as the wings of swans. When Etain sang in her high, sweet voice, the fairy folk said her song rivaled the harps of heaven. Etain was beloved by all—all, that is, but Femnach.

Femnach, the witch woman, hated Etain. She hated her voice and her beauty. More than anything else Femnach hated the goodness of Etain's soul.

One day, Femnach heard the sweet sound of Etain's singing. Concealing herself deep within her dark cloak, Femnach followed Etain into the forest.

Etain waded into a little stream. She stood in a shaft of sunlight, singing a happy song. To Femnach, Etain looked like a magical bird. Her gown of purple silk was shot through with weavings of red and silver and gold. Her blue and green cloak was fastened at the shoulder with a brooch of gold. Femnach could no longer bear Etain's beauty or the sweet magic of her song. Suddenly, she had a wicked idea. Femnach raised her hands and cast a spell.

> *"Etain, become a creature of the air.*
> *Fly far from Midir:*
> *Fly far from Eire.*
> *No song for comfort,*
> *No rest from care."*

Femnach watched, hoping that Etain would become an ugly black crow with its rasping caw. But even under the spell of Femnach's evil, Etain's beauty shone through. Before Femnach's eyes, Etain was transformed into a beautiful butterfly. Her blue and green wings shimmered with markings of purple, red, silver, and gold. Nor could Femnach take away Etain's lovely voice, for when Etain flapped her butterfly wings, they made a humming sound sweeter than the harps of heaven.

Now Femnach was terrified.

"The people of the Sidhe will know her!" she cried. "Midir will know her, if only by her song!"

So Femnach raised a wind that came beneath the butterfly's wings. It lifted Etain higher and higher until at last she reached the halls of heaven. There she landed on the palm of Aengus Og, keeper of the birds. Because Aengus knew all of the winged creatures of the world, he recognized Etain immediately.

"Alas," he cried. "Who has taken you away from Midir and the fairy folk?"

"Femnach the witch woman," Etain replied. "Can you send me back to my people?"

"I do not have the power to break this spell," Aengus said sadly, "but I can keep you safe with me in the halls of heaven."

So Aengus built Etain a crystal garden with trees of prisms and pearls and flowers like stained-glass windows in the sunlight. He brought her the finest honey and grasses and beseeched all the birds of heaven to keep the harsh winds away from her with the strength of their wings. There, in the garden of Aengus Og, Etain stayed for many years, humming such sad songs that it made Aengus weep to hear them.

Below, in the land of the Sidhe, Midir no longer threw back his head and laughed aloud. By the dark of night the fairy folk could hear him weeping for his lost Etain. By day he would don his white cloak, saddle his white horse, and ride to all the corners of Eire searching for his lost beloved.

Only Femnach was happy. She believed that Etain was dead.

One day Aengus Og had to travel to the world of the Sidhe.

"Take me with you," begged Etain. "Let me look just once more upon the people of the Sidhe and I will be able to sing joyful songs again."

Aengus Og could not resist such a promise, so he took Etain with him, resting lightly on his palm. When he reached Eire, he placed her gently on the petals of a red rose while he went about his business. So overjoyed was Etain to be among the roses of Eire that she began to hum a happy song.

Femnach was passing by and heard her.

"I believed that you were dead!" she cried. "Midir must not find you here."

Once again Femnach raised a wind, this one mightier than the first. It spun Etain past the world of the Sidhe, past the halls of heaven, far far east, into the world of humans.

Upon hearing the wind, Aengus Og returned and found Etain gone.

"What have you done?" he cried to Femnach.

When Femnach did not answer, Aengus knew that she had cast another spell on Etain. He grew very angry. He called to him all the birds of the world and they came swooping about the witch woman—gulls and eagles, hawks and crows—their wings flapping a terrible wind.

"Become what you wished for Etain!" cried Aengus Og.

Up and around spun the witch woman, trapped in the body of a black and ugly crow. Even now you can hear her cawing her anger at Aengus Og.

But Etain was gone.

For many days, the wind that Femnach had cast continued, buffeting Etain wildly above the world. Finally, after three long days, she fluttered to rest on the high broad beam of a castle ceiling.

Below her, the humans were having a feast. Their table was set with gold and crystal, piled high with sweets and honeyed bread. Etain was hungry and leaned forward to glimpse the feast. Just as she did, the wind caught at her again.

Down and down she spiraled, into the cup of the human queen. Just then, the queen lifted the wine to her lips and drank. Nine months later the queen gave birth to a beautiful baby daughter with hair the copper of autumn leaves and skin as white as the wings of swans. She named the child Etain.

Etain grew up gentle and kind, with a voice as sweet as the harps of heaven, but she no longer remembered Midir or that she was the queen of the fairy folk. Only her heart remembered, for each evening she would stand at the high tower window of the castle, looking off to the west. Then, she would sing such sad and longing songs that the humans would weep to hear them.

Etain's beauty brought many offers of marriage. At last, her parents decided to give her hand to young King Echu of Tara. Etain pleaded with them to change their minds.

"I do not belong with this man," she cried. "I will only bring him sorrow."

"Tell us then the man that you would choose," her mother replied.

Etain did not know and could not remember. In due time, Etain was married to Echu. Now, Echu admired Etain's great beauty and her lovely voice. He was as kind to her as a human king can be. But Echu's great love was his kingdom—his castles and horses and warriors and, most importantly, gold. He spent his hours fighting, riding, and counting his coffers of gold.

Each evening Etain stood alone and lonely at the high tower window, staring off to the west and singing such sad and longing songs that it made the people weep to hear them.

One evening when Etain was singing at her tower window, she saw a handsome young man in a white cloak, riding a white horse toward the castle. Immediately, Etain ceased her singing, her heart beating wildly within her, though she did not know why. She ran to the great hall to meet the stranger.

Midir, for he was indeed the rider, saw Etain coming down the great stair. For the first time in all his years of searching, he threw back his head and laughed aloud, a sound of so much joy that all the assembled people laughed with him.

"What can we give you, stranger?" Echu asked. "For you have made us glad of heart."

"One thing only," Midir replied. "I ask that you play me a game of fidchell. If you win, I will give you my bag of gold." He hefted a bag of gold onto the table and the bright coins spilled into the light. "But if I win the game, I ask but one kiss from your queen."

"One kiss is not so great a thing," said Echu, eyeing the gold. But he stared uneasily at Etain, who could not take her eyes from the stranger.

So they set up the patchwork board with its pieces of silver and gold and they played long into the flickering-firelight hours. At last, Midir won the game. When he stepped toward Etain to claim his prize, Echu changed his mind.

"Nay!" he cried. "She belongs to me. You shall not kiss her."

But Midir's lips had touched Etain's. In that moment she remembered all.

"Midir, my husband, my love," she cried. Then she burst into a song so joyful that it rivaled the harps of heaven.

When Echu heard the song, he knew that Etain would leave with Midir.

"Stop them!" he cried to his warriors. The warriors drew their swords and rushed toward the couple, but Midir threw his white cloak around Etain. In a sudden rush of wind, Midir and Etain disappeared. When Echu and his company ran outside the castle to search for them, Midir and Etain were nowhere to be found.

High above the castle tower two white swans circled against the starlit sky, then flew toward the west, far, far toward the magical country of the Sidhe.

The Ulster Cycle

In the first century B.C. in what we would now call Northern Ireland, there lived a clan called the Ulaid who were ruled by King Conchobar Mac Nessa. He ruled from the hill of Emain Macha (pronounced *Evin Maha*), near what is now Armagh. In his service was a great army known as the Red Branch. These were an interesting group of characters, to put it mildly. Conchobar himself has a patchwork story. At times he seems to be a wise ruler; at others, he does appalling things and abuses his power, as you will see in the chanted story below. Surely this is the saddest tale of the Ulster Cycle. Conchobar Mac Nessa, upon a dire prediction by a druid, walls a child up in a tower in the forest with only a nursemaid for company. The child is named Deirdre; Conchobar visits her throughout her childhood and, as she grows into a beautiful young woman, determines that he wants her for himself. Deirdre, however, has no love for the old king, her captor. Instead she falls in love with Naoise (pronounced *Neeshee*), a wandering huntsman with hair as black as a raven's wing, lips as red as blood, and cheeks as white as snow. Together they run away. Conchobar pursues them all through Ireland and even into Scotland and eventually tricks them back with promises of forgiveness and a great feast. He kills Naoise and brokenhearted Deirdre kills herself by leaning out of a thundering chariot. Below is the story as it might well have been chanted by the ancient bards, in rhythm and rhyme.

Deirdre of the Sorrows
By Juilene Osborne-McKnight

Naoise, when they sent your blood to ground
I died; the dark king will not let me go
though I am silent, my hands between my knees.
I do not eat; my thin bones clatter
as yours must now do. Naoise!
The thought of you in ground batters my heart.
Oh gods! This small and lustful king!
I hide this blaze of anger
behind the copper curtain of my hair;
I leave it lank, unwashed. I cannot bear
to think how I would dress its length

in flowers, lie so pale along you,
make rhythm in the firelight,
beating on the taut-skinned drum of night,
shrouded in the tumble of my hair.
You gods! He thinks that I am his,
this selfish king. He raised me
in the tower for my breasts, my thighs;
not once in all my childhood
did he meet my eyes, ask to hear me sing.
I was to be his saddlehorse, broodmare,
his pleasure pony only.
On the day I saw you in the glade,
light dappling through the leaves,
your eyes so piercing blue, I knew.
You drank my gaze, asked me to sing
from the tower wall
that you might memorize the song,
carry it to Alba with you like a fairy charm.
You called my hair a waterfall of fire;
that was all. I never longed for anyone but you;
still I do. Oh why did we return across the water?
Their promises, their tricks: I am his sickness.
He woos me now as if I were a stripling girl
immured still in his forest tower
and not a wife made widow at his whisper,
his lust command. I have done all a woman can—
greasy locks, skeletal bones, no word
but for the moaning of your name,
Naoise. Yesterday he asked me
which I hated more, himself the king
or cruel Mac Durthact, whose swing,
whose bloody blade tore you from my side.
Love, I answered true. *Each of you
is equal in my loathing. Each I hate.*
I ate the words. Naoise, they made me strong.
King Conor thought about them long;
at last he ruled. *For one year
you have made a fool of me.
I pass you to Mac Durthact.*

See what your little tears will wring
from his dark warrior heart.
He will use you up, your will or no,
make of you the very hag
you play before me now.
He will return you to me then,
a little year but broken in,
a doe between two stags.
Eist Naoise. Hush!
Hear me whisper now:
They bring the chariot around.
They bind me to the wickerwork.
I will stand proud! I ate the words;
they made me strong. None but you
and I will hear how loud my heartbeat
at the place where the long road forks,
the great stone thrusts from the ground.
Eist! I will make no sound.
Love requires of me only that I lean aside.
How small a thing when you have died
keeping me behind you with your shield.
Naoise, they have washed my copper hair
and plaited it with flowers. Little hours
separate us now. I cannot come
a slippered bride, lovely to behold,
but I will come bold, love, bold.
I did not yield. I will not now.
The horses thunder side by side.
Just a little step aside, my head just so.
This my love will do.
Naoise mo ghra. For you.
Ah you.

Then too, the Red Branch army who served Conchobar Mac Nessa were themselves a perplexing group, because while they were tremendous warriors, they also suffered from labor pains.

Yes, you actually read that correctly: labor pains, for men.

The ancient legend, in brief, says that Macha Fleet Foot, one of the "guises" of the Morrigu, cursed the men of Ulster because they made her run a footrace when she was seven months pregnant with twins. She won the race, but she cursed the Red Branch so that they would suffer labor pains in the hour of Ulster's greatest need. This detail goes a long way toward explaining the famous saga of Ulster, the collection of tales known as the *Táin bó Cúailnge.*

The *Táin* is the story of a war between Ulster and the neighboring county of Connacht, whose ruler was Queen Medb. Queen Medb is another very interesting historical character. Married to King Ailill, she is nonetheless openly libidinous, a behavior of which he is well aware. She is also a warrior, a powerful queen, and a strong believer in one-upmanship. The story goes that Medb and Ailill are having pillow talk one evening when Ailill boasts that he had more and better possessions than Medb. Medb immediately orders that all of their possessions be brought before them for counting, and they count everything from drinking goblets to diadems.

Unfortunately, Medb comes up one bull shy of a match for her husband's wealth. Ailill, it seems, owns a magical white bull called Finnbennach, known for its prowess. Nothing will do but that Medb must have a matching magical bull. As it happens, in nearby Ulster is a farmer named Daire (pronounced *Dairy*—yes, really!) who owns a magical brown bull called Donn Cúailnge. Medb sends her lawyers to negotiate a one-year rental of the bull, which goes well until the evening after the contracts are signed, when one of her soldiers happens to tell one of Daire's retainers that if they hadn't contracted for the bull, Medb was prepared to take it by battle. An angry Daire rescinds the contract and dares her to try, and so begins a war that lasts for many, many years and results in the death of Ireland's first great hero, Cú Chulainn.

Now this is where the pains of labor come into play.

Because all of the Red Branch warriors are laid low by the curse for a good part of the story, the seventeen-year-old boy Cú Chulainn ends up fighting almost the whole war against Medb and her armies singlehanded. Fortunately, ancient Ireland had an honor code of hand-to-hand combat, so in much of the *Táin*, Cú Chulainn is going up against warrior after warrior on his own strength. However, his own strength is rather unusual.

Cú Chulainn's mother, Dechtire, is married to a warrior named Sualtim; however, some time early in the marriage she is stolen away by Lugh, whom we know well at this point. The boy who is born of their mating is named Sétanta. When he is just twelve years old the family is invited to the rath of a blacksmith for dinner and while there, the boy runs down the road hitting his hurley ball (called a *sliotar*) with a stick. He strikes it so hard that it goes down the throat of the smith's dog, killing it.

As dogs were prized guardians in ancient Ireland, the smith is ready to kill the boy, but Sétanta volunteers to guard the blacksmith's rath for one year, until the blacksmith can train a new dog. He does such an extraordinary job of guarding the fort that he wins the love and respect of all the warriors and earns the name Cú Chulainn, the Hound of Ulster.

It soon becomes clear that guarding the fortress is not his only skill. The men of Ulster were tall in general, but Cú Chulainn is short with a bulbous nose and wild, frizzy red hair that forms a halo around his head. However, when he goes into battle, that appearance changes. He grows to nine feet tall, blood spurts from his forehead, one of his eyes bulges from its socket, his head can turn 360 degrees like the head of an owl, and his barbed spear, the *gae bulga*, which he throws with his foot, never misses.

Once he enters this war spasm or *riastradh*, he cannot be defeated and is impossible to calm down. One very funny story tells of how the only thing that can pacify him is being immersed in an icy-cold lake with hundreds of naked maidens!

Obviously, Cú Chulainn is not an ordinary young man, which is fortunate for Ulster because he defends them honorably and repeatedly, despite all of the tricks and warriors that Medb throws his way.

Medb has seven sons of her own and one daughter, named Finnabair. At one point, her warriors begin to turn her down when she asks them to go into single combat with Cú Chulainn, for obvious reasons. In order to sweeten the pot, Medb decides to auction off that daughter to any warrior who can defeat Cú Chulainn. While this certainly does not flatter Medb's mothering skills, it does fire the fictional imagination. Read, below, the fictional account of the first meeting between Finnabair and Cú Chulainn.

When last I had encountered him, my terror had been so great that nothing had registered but watery fear. But now I could see him clear in morning light. I shook my head in disbelief. This was the warrior all of my kinsmen feared, the one they called The Hound, the name which sent shivers through the men of Connacht? The man for whose death I had been sold into marriage . . .

Cuchulainn.

He seemed too young to carry upon his shoulders all the warriors of Ulster. And yet, that was what he did, for all of the Ulstermen suffered under a curse that rendered them unable to fight or even to rise up at certain times of the year. Momentarily, I wondered how such a curse had come upon them and by whom. I had never asked my mother, having no interest in the life of a warrior. And yet, she had based her whole war strategy around this curse somehow, sending warrior after warrior against this boy on the rock. I shook my head in incomprehension. How foolish it had all seemed to me. Until I was made a pawn in the war game. Now I wished that I knew all. I looked again at the boy on the rock.

Much upon my own years, he was still at least a head shorter than I. How had I not noticed that before? His body was dense and compact, as though a man's height had been crumpled down into a boy's frame. This made him bulky. Thick bands of muscle rippled across his abdomen and flexed in his legs when he stood, which he now did periodically, to throw what looked like bones toward the riverbank. His arms were thick and heavy and no bone missed its mark.

When he lowered himself to a sitting position again, he seemed to simply fold down, as fog curls around the base of a mountain. He resumed picking at whatever bird or game he was eating with obvious delight, chewing and chuckling aloud. Where had he come by food? Surely he had not left the rock in all the hours I had watched him.

How strange he was to look upon. His red-gold hair curled around his head in springy tight whorls. Evidently no artifice was needed to achieve this bizarre effect, for periodically the wind would pick up the hair, move it about, realign it in some wild new pattern. It looked like so much sprung milkweed, and I doubted that a comb had ever passed through it.

And then his face. It was broad and heavy, with double chins and a bulbous nose. I had heard stories that the women of Ulster admired him, vied for his attentions, offered him their services. Did they do so with their eyes closed?

My hand strayed to my own shorn locks and I felt a hot blush of shame creep up my face. What was I doing, after all? Would he remember me?

He started to whistle. The sound was captivating; perfect birdcalls issued from his mouth. Perhaps that was his appeal, then. Sound and not sight.

He stopped.

The Fenian Cycle and the Cycle of Kings

The Fenian and Kings cycles intersect between the third and fourth centuries A.D. and feature the exploits of the great high king of Ireland Cormac Mac Art and his consummate warrior, leader of the Fenians of Ireland, Fionn Mac Cumhail. This period is a golden age of ancient Ireland. Writings about Cormac Mac Art state that he was a wise king and provident ruler; during his forty-year reign, it is said that no one had to bar the door or guard the flock. Legend has it that he ruled with his four wolf brothers always beside him.

Cormac rebuilt the Hill of Tara, which had a tendency to burn down. He built a sun house for the women and their children, a huge school, a 750-foot-long banqueting hall lavishly decorated with hammered-metal screens, and a huge barracks for his Fenian army. From the air it is possible to see the outlines of a great rampart on that hill, but none of these fabled buildings survives.

According to legend, Cormac was the first Irish king to accept Christianity. He also supposedly wrote three books in his retirement (which was forced upon him when he lost his eye in a melee). These books were the *Teagasc an Riogh* (*Instructions of a King*), which contained precepts of wise rulership; the aforementioned *Book of Acaill*, which contained the brehon law; and the *Psalter of Tara,* which codified the history and genealogy of Ireland.

The Fenians were Cormac Mac Art's standing army. In peacetime, they numbered about nine thousand, but they swelled to twenty thousand in times of war. A basic unit of the Fenian army was the *fian,* which consisted of either six or twelve members. Fenians were divided into "battalions" of three thousand each.

Their leader was Fionn Mac Cumhail. No one knows if he was a real person or a legend, but he is the prototype for King Arthur and his sword. In fact, Fionn's sword, *In Cadabolg,* is the prototype for Excalibur. He required that his warriors live by a strict code of honor; even getting into the Fenian army was extremely difficult. Warriors had to leap into a waist-high pit and fend off arrow after arrow, armed only with a small forearm shield. Next they had to braid their hair and run barefoot through a forest, neither breaking a twig beneath their feet nor catching a branch in their hair, all while being chased by other warriors. Then, they had to recite from memory twelve long epic poems, because Fionn believed that a warrior could not be wise unless he knew his country's past. Finally, he had to declare himself *ecland agus dithir*—clanless and landless. His family became, de facto, the Fenian army.

The warriors lived by a code of honor. In the winter, they billeted in the villages of Ireland; for that privilege they provided both wood and meat. In summer they dwelled in the forests, living by hunting and fishing and sleeping in three-sided lean-tos called *bothies*. They were required to be excellent stewards of the land, leaving no sign of their passing—down to the ashes of their fire. In wartime, they were required to respect women and children. Rape was not tolerated, and if a child was orphaned during war, the Fenian who orphaned him was obligated to find him a suitable foster family. Each warrior also had a *geis,* or taboo, that forbade him from doing something. Like a Lenten fast, some warriors could not eat deer or boar, others could only drink on certain occasions, and so on. These *geasa* are the source of dozens of stories within the Fenian Cycle, which contains hundreds of stories. There were women among the warriors as well, some fighting in battles, others guarding seacoast towers or serving as runners between encampments.

Interestingly, one of the sources of Fionn's wisdom was the "salmon of knowledge." The story of how he gained that wisdom—accidentally—from a wizard is told below.

> *Fionn Mac Cumhail had walked upriver for three days searching for Finegas the wizard, the teacher his grandmother had sent him to find.*
>
> *On the third day when the sun was almost at the middle of the sky he saw an old, old man standing by the river with a fish spear in his hand. The ancient was muttering to himself until he saw Fionn.*

"Come, boy," he called. "Do you fish?"

Fionn felt surprised to be addressed so by a stranger, but he answered politely, "I do. May I be of service to you?"

"I tremble too much to spear him. Old man's palsy. Faugh! But there is a fish I must have. I have seen him today. A salmon. Big." He spread his hands apart, the spear in one hand.

The old man handed Fionn the spear.

"Do not touch him when you spear him," he said, wagging his finger. "Bring him straightaway to me."

Hours passed, but at last Fionn caught the fish, who sparkled like a rainbow in the setting of the sun. The old man clapped his hands.

"This is good work, boy. For ten years I have tried to catch him. Ten years! You came along just at the right time."

Fionn studied the old man, a suspicion forming in his mind. The old man's hair was all white; no gray remained in it. His face was like a dried apple, curved and curled upon itself. His white beard cascaded down his chest. He wore a white tunic embroidered in gold. He handed Fionn the fish, neatly skewered.

"Boy! I need you to turn this fish. Hear me good, boy. This fish cannot burn. There can be no burns or blisters on it. Do you hear me?"

Fionn nodded. He thought the man a little mad.

Fionn turned the fish carefully but at last a blister appeared on the skin of the fish. What to do? The old man had expressly told him not to allow the fish to burn. Fionn licked his thumb and pressed it hard against the blister. The blister disappeared from the skin of the fish, but now Fionn's finger throbbed.

He saw the old man coming toward him across the yard.

"I need to stop for just a moment," he called to the old man. "I have burned my thumb."

"No!" the old man shouted, waving his arms at Fionn, but Fionn had already lifted the burned thumb to his mouth and began to suck on it.

What he felt at first surprised him.

The air breathed. The light breathed. He felt dizzy and light and strange.

He stumbled and sank to his knees in the grass beside the river.

Past and present spun out before him and all the answers were clear.

He looked up to see the old man beating his fist against his palm in frustration.

"Father Finegas," he said, certain now of all that would come. "I am Fionn, come to learn the knowledge you are keeping for me."

The Story in Our Bones

And so we meet the most ancient of our ancestors—a people who organize their lives totally around the clan; a race of strong, empowered women; a society of warriors who are obsessed with the law; a people of deep spirituality, storytellers all, gathered at the feasting table. If they sound familiar, if you recognize these ancient forebears in your own family, in your own life, in your own work, at your own table, you should not be surprised. Their habits and characteristics travel in that most ancient of rivers—your genes.

As we will see in upcoming chapters, those characteristics are often the very things that saved our ancestors, that enabled them to prevail when they were sore beset. We call upon those same characteristics now, thousands of years down the pike, in another country. How we came to that country will be the subject of our upcoming chapters, as we look at the changes that our ancestors adopted and those that were imposed upon them.

For Further Reading: An Annotated Bibliography

Nonfiction

Barnes, Ian. *The Historical Atlas of the Celtic World.* New York: Chartwell Books, 2011.

This book is a map-lover's dream that puts every phase of Celtic history, from Gallic encounters with Hannibal to the Irish rising, on a map of the world at the time. In each section, the author clearly contextualizes the map with the events of the time.

Cunliffe, Barry. *The Ancient Celts.* London: Penguin Books, 1999. First published 1997 by Oxford University Press.

This scholarly book from a respected expert looks at the entire Celtic world, from archeological digs to communities remaining after Caesar. It gives excellent perspectives on the Celtic mindset and "mythset" and is replete with photos, timelines, and maps.

———. *The Celtic World.* New York: McGraw-Hill, 1979.

This lavishly illustrated coffee-table book is an extremely well organized and informative study of the world of the Celts. Cunliffe, a Celtic scholar, organizes the book by society, religion, art, destiny, island Celts, and modern Celts.

Delaney, Frank. *The Celts.* Boston: Little, Brown, 1986.

RTE and BBC broadcaster (and novelist) Frank Delaney wrote this book as a companion piece to a BBC television series on the Celts. The book is clear, well organized, illustrated, and informative, but in addition, Delaney, who is a consummate storyteller, roots it in a series of Irish stories that are formative to the Irish psyche.

Ellis, Peter Berresford. *The Ancient World of the Celts.* New York: Barnes & Noble Books, 1998.

Berresford Ellis organizes this book in a most accessible format. Rather than working chronologically, he organizes by classes of Celtic society such as druids, warriors, and women. In this fashion he gives the reader access to customs, beliefs, and material culture such as weapons or clothing.

——. *The Celtic Empire: The First Millennium of Celtic History 1000 B.C.—51 A.D.* Durham, NC: Carolina Academic Press, 1990.

Here Berresford Ellis focuses entirely on the Celtic world prior to the conquest of Britain by Rome.

Green, Miranda J., ed. *The Celtic World.* Oxford: Routledge, 1995.

The strength of this massive tome is the fact that each section contains essays by the best scholars, archeologists, and anthropologists in the Celtic world, each of whom provides additional references.

James, Simon. *The Atlantic Celts: Ancient People or Modern Invention?* London: British Museum Press, 1999.

This interesting little monograph is the source of much controversy because it questions all of the previous assumptions about the insular Celts of England and Ireland and their origins in both time and place. It is useful for the well-versed reader who wants to consider the counter-arguments.

Moscati, Sabatino, Otto Hermann Frey, Venceslas Kruta, Barry Raftery, and Miklos Szabo, eds. *The Celts.* New York: Rizzoli, 1991.

This book was published as a companion to a huge Celtic museum exhibition in Venice and "huge" also describes the book, which is lavishly illustrated with ancient Celtic artifacts and gives a thorough overview of the field of Celtic studies.

O'Kelly, Michael J. *Early Ireland: An Introduction to Irish Prehistory.* Cambridge: Cambridge University Press, 1989.

Archeologist O'Kelly focuses on Ireland from the Ice Age all the way through the Neolithic, Mesolithic, Bronze, and Iron ages. The book is thoroughly illustrated with maps and with photographs of archeological finds.

Sykes, Brian. *Saxons, Vikings and Celts: The Genetic Roots of Britain and Ireland.* New York: W. W. Norton, 2007.

This book is written by a geneticist from Oxford and, thus, analyzes genetic strains in England, Ireland, Scotland, and Wales, finding Anglo-Saxon and Viking pockets but less relationship to the Celts of the continent (i.e., France) than to a group who migrated from Spain (therefore intersecting nicely with the Irish myth of the Milesians).

Myth — Scholarly

Curran, Bob. *The Dark Spirit: Sinister Portraits from Celtic Folklore.* London: Cassell, 2001.

Stephen King has nothing on these ancient Celtic creepy-crawlies, which are drawn from the whole Celtic island world of Britain, Wales, Scotland, and Ireland and even the U.S. However, Bob Curran does not tell these tales as a storyteller but rather explains them as a folklorist, contextualizing them in myth and culture.

Dames, Michael. *Mythic Ireland.* London: Thames & Hudson, 1992.

Think of this book not as a collection of tales but rather a travel guide to mythic and early Christian sites in Ireland. Dames does an interesting job of connecting ancient customs and stories to the places where they occurred.

Ní Bhrolcháin, Muireann. *An Introduction to Early Irish Literature.* Dublin: Four Courts Press, 2009.

This book studies archetypes—or patterns—in early Irish storytelling as well as giving excellent summaries of the primary stories in the cycles. It is a very useful text for those who want to understand the tales in the context not only of history and culture but of storytelling tradition.

Rutherford, Ward. *Celtic Mythology: The Nature and Influence of Celtic Myth—from Druidism to Arthurian Legend.* New York: Sterling, 1990.

Rutherford works to contextualize ancient Celtic storytelling by archetype, geography, belief systems, culture, and style.

Slavin, Michael. *The Ancient Books of Ireland.* Ireland: Wolfhound Press, 2005.

This book is a must-have for every Celtophile's library because it summarizes and contextualizes the most ancient Irish manuscripts: *The Books of the Dun Cow, Ballymote, Lismore,* and *Durrow* as well as the brehon laws. Plus, the book is well organized, clearly explained, and beautifully illustrated.

Myth—Collections of Stories

Cross, Tom P., and Clark Harris Slover. *Ancient Irish Tales.* New York: Barnes & Noble Books, 1996. First published 1936.
Although the language is somewhat stilted, this is an extensive collection of stories from all Four Cycles of storytelling.

Curtin, Jeremiah. *Myths and Folklore of Ireland.* New York: Wings Books. First published 1890.
These are stories collected by a folklorist who traveled in the Gaeltachta (the places where Irish is still spoken). They are not organized by cycle and include myths, folktales, fairytales, and more, but the stories have an authentic, old-fashioned sound.

Delaney, Frank. *Legends of the Celts.* New York: Sterling, 1991.
Delaney, a wonderful storyteller, tells tales from the Mythic and Ulster cycles and then shifts to Welsh mythology.

Glassie, Henry, ed. *Irish Folk Tales.* New York: Pantheon, 1985.
This wonderful collection, by an American folklorist and professor, of folk, fairy, ghost, and wit stories from throughout Ireland and its history, is a favorite of the author.

Lenihan, Eddie, and Carolyn Eve Green. *Meeting the Other Crowd: The Fairy Stories of Hidden Ireland.* New York: Putnam, 2003.
This is a collection of gems, some funny, some scary, about encounters with the Sidhe throughout Ireland and its history. Many of the stories are enhanced by first-person commentary from the author on their origins and the people who told them. It is a real delight.

Matthews, Caitlín. *Celtic Love: Ten Enchanted Stories.* San Francisco: Harper, 2000.
Each of these wonderful tellings of love stories from Ireland, Wales,

Scotland, and Britain is prefaced with its history and liberally salted with bardic-style poetry.

Matthews, John. *Classic Celtic Fairy Tales.* London: Blandford Press, 1997.
This most unusual collection of tales from all of the Celtic Isles is beautifully illustrated by Ian Daniels. Matthews gives background notes on each story and its origins, something that storytellers very much appreciate, and these stories are wonderfully told.

Monaghan, Patricia. *The Red-Haired Girl from the Bog.* Novato, CA: New World Library, 2003.
This is a fascinating, first-person study of ancient pre-Christian religious sites and beliefs still extant in Ireland. Written in lovely, essay style, it is beautifully descriptive and humorous.

Rolleston, T. W. *The High Deeds of Finn.* New York: Lemma, 1973.
Because Rolleston focuses on Fionn and Cormac Mac Art, this is an excellent sourcebook for the Fionn cycle.

Ross, Anne. *Druids, Gods & Heroes from Celtic Mythology.* New York: Peter Bedrick Books, 1986.
This book with gorgeous illustrations by Roger Garland and line drawings by John Sibbick tells stories of Cú Chulainn, Fionn, the Welsh Mabinogion, and King Arthur.

Scott, Michael. *Irish Folk & Fairy Tales Omnibus.* London: Sphere Books, 1989.
Three volumes of Scott's well-told tales are collected here in one large edition.

——. *Irish Ghosts and Hauntings.* London: Sphere Books, 2008.
This collection of scary stories is well told.

Yeats, W. B., and Lady Gregory. *A Treasury of Irish Myth, Legend and Folklore.* Edited by Claire Booss. New York: Gramercy Books, 1986.
This is the original collection of stories from the Celtic Twilight, the movement to revive ancient Irish stories and art started by Yeats and Lady Gregory and carried into the Abbey Theater. The book contains a large selection of folk- and fairytales that Yeats and Lady Gregory and

their cohorts collected from the field; some of those are from the Four Cycles and others are more modern. It also contains Lady Gregory's translation of the *Táin bó Cúailnge,* which does not include all of the stories and "cleans up" some of the more earthy tales. However, it is a collection worthy of respect because the entire movement did so much to preserve the ancient Celtic stories.

Zaczek, Iain. *Chronicles of the Celts.* New York: Sterling, 1996.
This book contains tales from three of the Four Cycles, Welsh and Breton tales, nice illustrations and photographs, and contextual sidebars.

———. *Irish Legends.* New York: Barnes & Noble Books, 2002.
Zaczek tells stories from the Mythological, Ulster, and Fionn cycles. The tales are accompanied by historical context and good photographs.

Fiction

There is an abundance of Celtic fiction on Arthurian myth, Celtic Britain, Welsh myth, etc., and no lack of fantasy fiction based in Celtic mythology, including by such greats as J. R. R. Tolkien, but the fiction listed here resides firmly and deliberately in Irish history and myth from the periods we have discussed in this chapter.

Eickhoff, Randy Lee
A former professor and author of dozens of books, Eickhoff has done a multibook translation of the *Táin bó Cúailnge.*
- *The Raid*
- *The Feast*
- *The Destruction of the Inn*
- *He Stands Alone*
- *The Sorrows*
- *The Red Branch Tales*

Flint, Kenneth C. [Casey Flynn]
Flint/Flynn is a fantasy author who writes books based in ancient Irish mythology. These books are currently out of print, but they are well worth a search online.
Flint's Fionn Mac Cumhail series

- *Challenge of the Clans*
- *Storm Shield*
- *The Dark Druid*

Flint's Sidhe series

- *The Riders of the Sidhe*
- *Champions of the Sidhe*
- *Master of the Sidhe*
- *Heart of the Sidhe*

Kinsella, Thomas. *The Táin.* Oxford: Oxford University Press, 2002. This is a brilliant translation.

Llywelyn, Morgan

Morgan Llywelyn is the high priestess of Celtic historical fiction. She draws in-depth characters while also teaching the reader about the customs and history of the time period in which the novels are set.

- *Bard: The Odyssey of the Irish.* New York: Tor, 1984. The story of the Milesian migration to Ireland.
- *Druids.* New York: William Morrow, 1991. The demise of the Gauls (the Celts of France) under Julius Caesar, as seen through the eyes of Vercingetorix and his druid Ainvar.
- *Finn Mac Cool.* New York: Forge, 1994. Story of the hero of the Fenian Cycle.
- *The Greener Shore.* New York: Del Rey Books/Random House, 2006. Ainvar and a group of Gauls flee France for Ireland.
- *Red Branch.* New York: William Morrow, 1989. The story of Cú Chulainn.

Osborne-McKnight, Juilene

The author of the book that you are currently reading is also the author of four novels set in early Ireland.

- *Bright Sword of Ireland.* New York: Forge, 2005. The story of Finnabair, daughter of Queen Medb of Connaught, auctioned off by her mother.
- *Daughter of Ireland.* New York: Forge, 2003. Story of the druidess Aislinn ni Sorar and her quest to find the truth of her childhood.

- *I Am of Irelaunde.* New York: Forge, 2001. The story of Osian, son of Fionn Mac Cumhail, juxtaposed against the story of St. Patrick.
- *Song of Ireland.* New York: Forge, 2006. The story of the coming of the Milesians to Ireland and their encounter with the little people, the Sidhe of Ireland.

Video

"Caesar Super Siege." Season 1, Episode 4. *Battles B.C.* DVD. Directed by David Padrusch. A&E Home Video, 2009.

Filmed in a style similar to that of the film *300,* this episode does an excellent job of breaking down Caesar's war against the Gauls, his defeat of Vercingetorix, and his military tactics.

The Celts. DVD. Directed by David Richardson. BBC Home Entertainment, 2013.

Written and hosted by Frank Delaney, these six truly fascinating episodes explore Celtic origins, beliefs, and cultural survival in Ireland and Britain.

The Celts: The Complete Epic Saga. DVD. Kultur Video, 2010.

This series, an Opus Television production for S4C International/Rhyngwladol, grounds the viewer in the history of the continental Celts, Celtic languages, wars, defeat by Caesar, religious beliefs, etc. It also examines the historicity or myth of King Arthur.

Keeping Faith at the Crossroad
Celtic Christianity

Part II: Keeping Faith at the Crossroad: Celtic Christianity

5
Druids First, Christians Later: Druidic Beliefs

To understand Irish Christianity, you must first understand druidry, for two good reasons:

1) For a very long time, Christianity in Ireland was interwoven with previous pagan belief systems, as you will see in this chapter, and

2) Druids were often early converts to Christianity and became monks and priests in the early Church. Why? Because philosophically, they were not as different as it might appear at first blush.

Most importantly of all for our purposes, however, you are about to learn something truly surprising. If you are Irish and Catholic, the form of Christianity that your ancestors practiced—all the way through the Middle Ages—was as different from Roman Christianity as military school is from dance class.

How? And why did it change so radically? These are the questions that we will answer.

Druids, as you might remember, were the professors of ancient Ireland. Roman writers tell us that they were divided into three groups: druids, ovates, and bards. While that might simply be a conqueror's impression, druids were certainly the highest-level members of the aos dána, the learned class of Ireland that included poets, bards, lawyers, physicians, genealogists, and, at the top of the list, druids.

To become a druid, a man or woman had to study for twenty years, and the impressive volume of their "coursework" could never be saved on a hard drive or written in a journal. Instead, they carried their knowledge in their heads. Druids would have been familiar with philosophy, eventually including Greek and Roman thinking. They would have known the history of Ireland, genealogy, meteorology, agriculture, poetry, and storytelling.

Elder druids would have served as teachers, not only inculcating novices into the order but teaching the young children of Ireland in the great schools of the higher Irish chiefs, such as the Teach Forradh of Cormac Mac Art at the Hill of Tara.

When it came to sacred ritual, the "buck stopped" at the desk of the druids. They performed them in oak groves called *fidnemid* in Ireland and *nemeton* on the continent. These groves were populated by massive oak trees, considered sacred because their arms are always lifted in an attitude of prayer and because their great age represented wisdom. Often, in Ireland, these oak groves were surrounded by thick hedges of thorny blackthorn bushes, so that the uninitiated would not stumble into sacred ceremonies. Here, among the towering trees, the druids would pray, listen, divine for answers, and sometimes perform

Many scholars of the Celtic world believe that Chartres Cathedral, left, sits on the most central of druid sacred sites in Gaul, in the territory of the tribe called the Carnutes. Indeed, there is an ancient well in the crypt of the cathedral (above) known as the druid well.

sacrifices. It will help us to understand what they believed and what rituals they practiced, as far as we know, because in their belief systems are the seeds for Ireland's acceptance of Christianity.

Druidic Beliefs and Practices

- Sacred ceremonies were conducted by moonlight. One of these was the cutting of the mistletoe. Roman historian Pliny the Elder tells us that on the sixth day of a waxing moon, the druids held a ritual feast under the oak trees, then cut the mistletoe with a golden knife and dropped it into a white cloak, after which they sacrificed two white bulls. We don't know how accurate this description of their ceremony is, but we do know the following:

  - Sacrifice of bulls was common in the Celtic world (and in the Roman army, as we will see later). Bulls symbolized power and fertility, and their sacrifice signaled a major offering to the gods.
  - The Celts did indeed reckon time by the moon.
  - High druids often wore lunula, hammered golden torcs that looked like crescent moons. Several of these are on display in the National Museum of Ireland on Kildare Street in Dublin.
  - Feasting was the central celebratory and sacred event of Irish life.
  - Although mistletoe is poisonous, there are historical references to its use as a cure for cancer. In a strange modern twist, *Johns Hopkins Magazine* recently ran an article about their oncology staff injecting mistletoe compounds into a patient with liver cancer as a treatment.

The Druids Cutting the Mistletoe on the Sixth Day of the Moon, by French painter Henri-Paul Motte. Oil on canvas circa 1890. (Used here by licensing arrangement with Bridgeman Images, London and New York)

The Druids Bringing in the Mistletoe, by George Henry and Edward Atkinson Hornel, 1890. The original hangs in the Glasgow Museum. (Used here by licensing arrangement with Bridgeman Images, London and New York) Note the golden sickle in the hands of the chief druid, as well as the majestic oak trees. Note also the presence of women in the company; as in all other aspects of Irish life, women were accepted into druidic training.

Perhaps the druids knew something then that has been long forgotten.

- The druids taught that every human being possesses a soul. That soul continued after death. They believed that the soul resided in the head.

  - This led to a very unusual practice in Celtic Ireland. Warriors collected the heads of their enemies in battle. They were cleansed, preserved with special oils, and kept in decorated boxes or even displayed on shelves in a home. Horse warriors often strung those heads on chains attached to their saddles when they rode into battle, because they believed that the spirits of these vanquished enemies would protect them.

- Because the Celts believed in their own continuation after death, they were unusually fearless about death, a fact that both perplexed and astonished the Romans.

  - The Celts saw death as a temporary state. It was often spent among the Others in an island paradise, variously called *Tir-nan-Og, Hy-Brasil,* or Land of the Ever Young. There, time passed differently than it did on earth and there was no pain. Everyone was youthful and healthy and spent their time feasting, singing, and dancing.

- Because the Irish believed that death was essentially just a transition between lives, funerals were often occasions of feasting and joy and births quite solemn. Druids would thank the newborn infant for choosing to return, despite the challenges of life.

- As we have discussed, the Celts believed in numerous tripartite gods and goddesses. In fact, three was the sacred Celtic number. However, dozens of individual gods and goddesses were associated with a place, concept, or set of skills.

  - Brighid/Anu/Dana were goddesses of the light forces such as childbirth, fire, and poetry, while Macha/Banbh/Nemhain sowed war and chaos and feasted on the carrion of battlefields. Such beliefs tell us that the ancient Irish had a very clear sense of the duality of human nature, i.e., of good and evil.
  - Gods such as Ogma, the honey mouthed, helped people with elegance of speech, while Boann was the goddess attached to the Boyne River. Manannan Mac Lir was the god of the sea. Belief in all of these deities helped to explain natural phenomena and led to the profound Irish sense that place is sacred.
  - We do know that the druids used sacrifice in rituals, in particular sacrifice of bulls and mares. Roman historians say that they sacrificed humans in huge wicker men, but there is no evidence of this and such structures would have been engineering nightmares. Most scholars today think such spectacles were not likely. However, druids did sometimes sacrifice humans in very ritual ways, and many scholars believe that sacrificial victims were highly honored. For example, Lindow Man, who was found in a bog in England, had burned bread in his stomach and had been hit on the head, garroted, and then had his throat cut. What god was being propitiated or petitioned with this ritual is unknown, but if the subject fascinates you, you should read *The Life and Death of a Druid Prince,* by archeologist Anne Ross and chemist Don Robins.

- The druids taught that many places, certain times, and even various animals were liminal. In other words, the Celtic worldview was that all of creation could offer "doorways" through which a human being could directly experience the spirit world.

- Water was almost always a doorway. In the Celtic worldview, wells, waterfalls, and lakes served as portals between this world and the spirit world.
- Standing stones and dolmens were also thought of as doorways.
- Changes of seasons and changes from light to darkness or darkness to light could open doorways.
- Druids also thought that they could learn to shapeshift. Thus, a druid who had prepared well could see the world through the eyes of an owl, eagle, fish, wolf, or bear. Interestingly, one of the best examples of this Celtic way of thinking occurs in the animated Disney movie *The Sword in the Stone,* in which Merlin teaches young Arthur (Wart) to understand creation from the perspective of fish and squirrels.

- Words were extremely powerful in druidic perception. Neither history nor sacred knowledge was written down;everything was committed to memory. This was not because ancient Irish society was "illiterate." Rather, the druids realized that knowledge is power, and that power must be guarded.

  - *Glam dicen*—or ritual curse—was a weapon so strong that if a poet leveled it at an enemy, that person might break out in boils or die from the force of the words.
  - *Rosc,* a poem of praise, would elevate its subject throughout the whole society.
  - If a druid or poet walked into the middle of a battlefield and declared the war over, it would stop immediately.

In many of these ancient beliefs and customs you can already see the obvious connections to Christianity—the belief in tripartite gods, in the soul, in a "heavenly" life after death. One can see how Christianity would resonate with such a spiritual culture, who would have no problem understanding "in the beginning was the Word. . . ."

Modern Druids Among Us

Here at Blenheim Palace in England, Winston Churchill was inducted into the Albion Lodge of the Ancient Order of Druids in August of 1908. This massive estate was the residence of the Dukes

of Marlborough, a title created in the 1700s for an early Churchill. Because Winston Churchill was a descendant, he was born at Blenheim Palace. His mother, Jennie Jerome (Lady Randolph Churchill), was an American heiress from Brooklyn.

The Ancient Order of Druids, which still exists, was founded as a secret fraternal organization that had nothing whatsoever to do with ancient druidry or anything religious, even though the lodge presidents, known as archdruids, did wear white robes and fake beards and carry big sticks.

Modern folks on both sides of the pond seem to have an ongoing fascination with druidry. Contemporary druidic groups often carry out ceremonies at megalith sites such as Stonehenge, although this is historically inaccurate. Construction of megalith sites began somewhere around 3800 B.C., long before druids or druidic practice existed in the British Isles.

Often, modern druids practice a seasonal wheel of rituals, with the aforementioned Samhain, Imbolc, Beltaine, and Lughnasa being the primary celebrations, spaced about three months apart. Some groups are neo-pagan and worship a variety of Pan-Celtic gods, while others see nature as sacred and practice environmental conservation, such as the Ancient Order of Druids in America, which supports such organizations as the Audubon Society. Many are nonreligious or accept members from a variety of religions.

Modern Druids

• The Order of Bards, Ovates and Druids is a very large group founded in Great Britain. Its adherents around the world ascend through the three grades of membership indicated in its name.

• The British Druid Order, founded in 1979, was brought to the United States in 1997. It is organized around ancient Welsh traditions and gods.

• The Reformed Druids of North America claim to be the largest druidic group on this side of the pond, with 3,500 members. It was founded by a group of undergrads who did not wish to attend required chapel services at Carleton College in Minnesota, but they grew larger and more seriously interested in neo-druidism.

• *Ár nDraíocht Féin* (meaning "Our Own Magic"), founded by Isaac Bonewits, is an American neo-pagan group.

6

Christianity Comes to Ireland

Many pagan customs persisted into Christian times. For example, the circle around the Irish cross above recognizes not only the eternal aspect of Christianity but the sun and the cyclical nature of life and death that was clear to our ancient ancestors. Even the cult of the head persisted into Christian times, with heads and sometimes skulls being carved into the stone recesses of a church, as you can see in the early Christian church in County Carlow above.

Most Americans believe that Christianity came to Ireland with St. Patrick. Why else would we dress up and drink green beer on March

17? In truth, however, by the time St. Patrick got to Ireland, somewhere around 431 or so, Christianity already existed in scattered pockets throughout the country. Historians are not sure how it arrived, but there was certainly extensive trading with Rome. Slavery, which was the norm at the time, may have been profoundly influential in spreading Christianity throughout Ireland. Ireland converted to Christianity without bloodshed. Not only did no one force the religion upon them, but the Irish also did not endure the mass martyrdoms that early Christians had endured under Rome. In truth, the Irish had all the paradigms in place to allow them to accept the new religion and to understand its profound mysticism and its tripartite God.

However, Christianity in Ireland was profoundly different from Roman Christianity—Rome may have believed that it was dangerously so. Pelagius, an Irish theologian, had spread his ideas of Christianity throughout Great Britain, Gaul, and Ireland. Augustine believed that man is born with original sin and can only be redeemed by grace, but Pelagius disagreed, saying that babies are born innocent and that sin is a choice of free will. Pelagius was excommunicated in 418 A.D., but his ideas had infiltrated the islands. Somewhere along the line, perhaps around 431 A.D., the Roman Church sent a bishop named Palladius to Ireland, likely with the mission to root out Pelagian heresy.

In point of fact, his mission was probably moot before it began. Irish Christianity developed so differently from Roman Christianity that Pelagius's ideas were only the tip of the iceberg. Remember that the Irish saw their land as holy, liminal, magical. Because they perceived everything as being imbued with spirit, they were panentheistic. Our ancestors observed no difference between myth and history. Myth was history; history myth.

The Roman Empire formally adopted Christianity under the Emperor Constantine, so of course it was placed in a Roman administrative framework. Christianity centered itself in Rome—certainly the power base of the ancient world. The Romans were amazing builders and organizers; however, their myths and indeed their gods were almost all borrowed from other cultures.

Rome was traditionally hierarchical. Popes, cardinals, archbishops, bishops, and priests had a definite pecking order. Rome wanted priests to be celibate and to follow Roman rule. The Irish were—and still are—the least hierarchical people on the face of the earth.

Plus, the position of women among the Irish was nothing like the position of women in Rome. Women had no roles in the Roman Church or in Roman government; by contrast, they were full players in the Irish Church.

Besides Palladius, several other early Christianizers figured in Irish history, such as Ibar, Declan, Ailbe, and Ciaran, but the saint whose personality dominates is St. Patrick. In part this is because his "biographers"—two monks named Tirechán and Muirchu, as well as many later hagiographers—mythologized Patrick into someone he never was: a man who fought with druids, used shamrocks to teach the trinity, and drove the snakes from Ireland. In truth, many druids became the priests of the new religion, Patrick surely didn't need shamrocks to teach a people who already had tripartite gods, and Ireland never had any snakes in the first place!

But we Americans also have ourselves to blame for a mythologized St. Patrick. Until recent years, St. Patrick's Day in Ireland was a simple observance, perhaps marked by a Mass. Not so in America; we are the ones who made St. Patrick's Day a wild, green bacchanalia of beer, leprechauns, and parades. Our New York parade is the largest in the world, in Chicago we dye the river green, and Savannah, Georgia counts down the days, hours, and minutes to their parade, which is always held on March 17 itself. We even aver that everyone is Irish on St. Patrick's Day.

Yet almost everything we know about St. Patrick is wrong!

St. Patrick: Story of Surprises

Most images of St. Patrick depict him capped by his green mitre and carrying his crozier. Draped in a green chasuble, he points to the snakes at his feet, all of which are fleeing Ireland. All of it is wrong and poor Patrick looks old, overdressed for traveling, and more than a little sappy.

St. Patrick's story—his real story—has come down to us in two documents, his *Confessio*, which is essentially his journal, and a letter that he wrote called *Letter to the Soldiers of Coroticus*. They tell a story that is not the least bit sappy; in fact, it would make a phenomenal movie, but the only movie on the subject is *St. Patrick: The Irish Legend* (2000), starring Patrick Bergin, which is full of laugh-out-loud inaccuracies (although the scenery is beautiful).

The Patrick who reveals himself in these writings is full of surprises.

First of all, he isn't Irish. St. Patrick is Romano/Welsh/Briton. He tells us that his grandfather's home was at Bannavem Taburniae. No such place is referenced in any historical documents that we can find, but scholars guess that it had to be either the seacoast of Wales or of southwest Scotland. Why? Because that is where Patrick was captured as a slave.

To our modern sensibilities, slavery is anathema, but in the ancient world, it was the way of the workforce. Some scholars estimate that the Roman Empire was fully two-thirds slaves! In the islands, the Scots, Welsh, Irish, and Britons raided each other constantly for slaves.

Imagine this. It is dark but sliding into predawn grey. The boy Patrick, son of a well-to-do Christian deacon named Calpurnius, grandson of a Catholic priest named Potitus (yes, his grandfather was married), is asleep in his bed. Up the river from the sea come the silent boats of King Niall of the Nine Hostages, one of the great Uí Néill kings of Northern Ireland. He and his warriors attack the settlement and drag the sleeping residents from their beds. Perhaps they leave the old and young alone; perhaps they are slaughtered. But Patrick is sixteen, young and strong. Along with thousands of others, according to his testimony, he is trussed up, thrown into the bottom of a boat, and taken to Ireland. There, naked and shivering, clapped into a slave collar, he is sold to a sheepholder at the far, wild side of Ireland in County Mayo. Only days before, he spoke Latin or Briton or both, was beloved by both his parents, ate well, lived in a rich villa heated by hypocausts in the floor, and had friends and extended family.

Now he speaks no Irish, he has no rights, and his collar marks him as a slave. He is given a tiny stone *clochan* or hut (which looks like an overturned boat), a herd of sheep, and some wolfhounds to help him manage the sheep. He is completely alone—for the rest of his life, for all he knows.

Oh my, he hates Ireland. And oh my, he hates the Irish. Can you blame him?

He tells us that he had not been a religious youth, despite the family pedigree, but all alone in the stony West, with only his huge dogs as his companions, he begins to pray. And oh, does he pray, he tells us—a hundred prayers a day and a hundred prayers a night.

He does that for six years.

Meanwhile, he is evidently befriended by residents of the nearby village called Foclut Wood (an actual place in County Mayo), and he learns to speak rudimentary Irish.

When he is twenty-two years old, he is awakened by a voice in the middle of the night. This voice will return to him over and over again throughout his life. "Behold," it says. "Your ship is ready."

What ship? He is in a stone field full of sheep somewhere in County Mayo.

Patrick then performs what must be considered one of the greatest acts of complete faith in the history of the world. Wearing his slave collar, escaping under threat of execution, he walks to where the ships are. He travels 250 miles to the docks near what we now call Dublin. He petitions a ship to take him home, but they decline; after all, the ships trade slaves, and he is clearly marked.

He tells us that he is terribly disappointed but returns to his hut. Shortly thereafter, the sailors find him and say that the captain has decided to take him on after all.

Why? We don't know. Perhaps they were shorthanded. While Patrick's own journal does not tell us this, legend says that the cargo of the ship was wolfhounds and that Patrick was able to walk among them and calm them, so he was granted passage. This would have been no mean feat in the ancient days, as wolfhounds were head and shoulders taller than a man and bred for the purpose of hunting and killing the wolves who stalked sheep. For storytelling sake, we can only hope that this part of the St. Patrick legend is true!

Patrick has a stunning adventure as he tries to return to Britain that involves getting lost, being threatened with death by hungry pagan sailors, and then praying up a herd of wild boar to feed them, topped off with wild honey. When he finally gets home, you can imagine his family's joy. Their child, who they thought was dead, has returned to them—six years older, careworn, and worldly wise, but alive. They beg him not to return to Ireland and Patrick is not of a mind to go back . . . ever.

And then the voice returns. In dreams, an angel named Victoricus brings him letters from the people of Foclut Wood, who beg him to come back to Ireland. Finally, at the age of forty, he returns.

It is important for us to take a sidebar moment to understand how our ancestors saw the world. To us, as Irish-Americans, we see the world in a Western, rational, scientific, give-me-proof sort of way. There is the real and the unreal. There is alive and there is dead. There is heaven and there is earth. In our worldview, those polar opposites do not touch. To our ancestors, they touched all the time—even right now.

We might have a little trouble believing that an angel would show up in a dream carrying letters. Our ancestors would have readily conversed with the angel. To them, the world was porous. They knew themselves to be spirit and they knew with certainty that their spirits were at best only a step away from the spirits of the dead and the messengers of God.

Over and over again in the stories of the saints, you will see doors open between the world of the natural and the world of the supernatural.

Before we scoff, with our modern minds, we might be wise to consider whether we have simply lost or abandoned our own ability to see and hear.

Patrick Returns to Ireland

You might have noticed that there was a gap in the story of Patrick. What happened to him between the ages of twenty-two and forty?

We don't really know. Some scholars say that Patrick went to Auxerre in France to train for the priesthood and be ordained a bishop. If so, he never really emerged as well educated, because he tells us in his own *Confessio* that his Latin is rude and ungrammatical.

Whatever the story of the gap, when Patrick returns to Ireland, it is likely that he lands in Armagh, somewhere between the years of 431 and 434 A.D. He converts a local chieftain named Dichu (again, according to legend, by calming the man's slobbering wolfhounds) and sets up his first church.

What we see in Patrick in his *Confessio* is a man of many parts. He is fiery and stubborn. He defends himself against accusations that he has done anything untoward, such as accepting financial gifts from his converts. He is embarrassed about the gap in his education. He is celibate, but he likes and respects women, converting many. When some of his converts are captured into slavery, as he had been, he fires off a scathing letter to their captor, Coroticus, and his warriors.

Patrick is real, complex, difficult, and as solid in his faith as he once was wishy-washy, but frustrated with the Church's bureaucracy and hierarchy. Read his journal if you have an evening; dozens of translations are available. You will like him and dislike him. You will find him hardnosed and practical at the same time that he is downright mystical.

In one section of his *Confessio,* he talks about a sin that he committed in his youth, a sin that he confesses to his *anam cara* (more about anam cara later) before he is to be ordained as a deacon. He tells us that he committed this sin when he was only fifteen, before he was kidnapped and taken away from Ireland. He says that the sin was an error of a single hour. However, his "friend" rats him out to the hierarchy, who then consider not ordaining him at all! How different the history of Ireland might have been if they had rejected Patrick.

Scholars have debated and debated the nature of this sin. Some say that it was sexual, but sexuality in Patrick's time was not really considered sinful unless it was forced, and many of the clergy were not celibate. Other scholars speculate that the sin might have been participation in a pagan ritual and this seems more likely, given how seriously the hierarchy of the Church took the confession. Patrick grew up in a Romanized area that was being abandoned by the Roman soldiery, who were being called back to the mother country. Many Romans practiced a pagan religion called Mithraism, based on a Persian boy god who slays a white bull, returns fertility to the harvest, and is rewarded with life in heaven. This was an appealing and hopeful religion for soldiers who were trained and paid to fight and die. Perhaps Patrick participated in one of their temple ceremonies. We will never know.

Most surprisingly, one has the feeling

Ruins of a Roman Mithraeum at Ostia Antica outside Rome.

that by the end of his life, Patrick has become "more Irish than the Irish," that he has come to love his converts and his adopted land. What he never did achieve, however, was any sense of converting the Irish to a Romanized version of Christianity. The Roman Empire boasted well-organized cities, with clear bureaucratic structures. Ireland was still living the life of the small, circular village—the ancient life of the rath. It was that life that determined the direction of Christianity in Ireland.

St. Patrick Converts the King of Cashel

Retold and adapted by Juilene Osborne-McKnight

Téann an scéal: *the story goes that Patrick and his monks wintered out on the rock of Cashel, with Angus, the high king of that country. All winter, they drank mead by the fire and traded stories, and when Imbolc came, Angus announced that he would take baptism in the new religion.*

Delighted, Patrick arrived at the crest of the hill in his bishop's robes, carrying his fine silver crozier with the sharp pointed end, but Angus came bare legged and bare armed, in a homespun tunic. When Patrick asked him why, Angus replied, "It seems to me your Christ was a simple man and this would do him honor."

Patrick was so impressed with this answer that he struck the ground three times with his crozier and cried out, "In the name of the Father, the Son, and the Holy Ghost." On the third strike he felt the crozier sink deep into the frozen ground.

Angus took the baptism with a look of agony on his face, and Patrick thought how hard it must be for the Irish chief to give up his old ways. When the baptism was over, Patrick clapped the great chief on the arms and welcomed him as a brother in Christ.

Angus, still gritting his teeth, leaned forward. "I thank you, brother," he whispered, "but when is it proper to take care of my foot?"

What Changed Patrick's Heart?

Remember that for the Irish, there is a myth to explain everything. They wondered how St. Patrick, who loathed the Irish, came to love them so, and out of that question arose one of the best of all Irish

View from the Rock of Cashel, stronghold of the Kings of Munster and the supposed location of the conversion story told opposite.

myths, the *Agallam na Seanorach,* the "Meeting of the Old Men." In this story, Osian, son of Fionn Mac Cumhail, returns from the Land of the Ever Young, where he has been living with his beloved wife, Niamh Golden Hair, who is a woman of the Sidhe—the Others. Osian wishes to see his father, Fionn, and his son, Oscar, but he is unaware that he has been among the Others for so long that everyone he knew is long gone.

His wife begs him not to set foot on the ground in Ireland, for she knows that if he does, he will return to human time, grow old, and die.

On the day Osian arrives, Patrick and his monks are planting in the garden of the church. They see a huge man astride a white horse; the passage below tells that story.

At the edge of the field, a man sat still as stone astride a white horse. His cloak of interwoven blue and green breacan moved like wings in the wind. He watched us, a sentinel, unmoving. From my distance, he looked young, his

7

Monastic Life in Ancient Ireland

The monastery at Glendalough ("Valley/Glen of the Two Lakes"), founded by St. Kevin sometime in the seventh century, became, as many monasteries did, a place of pilgrimage and later the site of an entire monastic city. Poor St. Kevin (*Caoimhín*, in Irish) went to the lakes because he just wanted some peace and quiet for contemplation, but followers searched him out there and built a little community. Kevin tried to avoid the responsibility of being a teacher; in fact, he hid out in a cave above the lakes for a while, but finally he had to give up and become an abbot in a Christian model that would define Irish life for centuries.

To understand the Christianity of our Irish ancestors, you need to understand a few core points about the early Irish converts.

- Early Irish priests, monks, and nuns were celibate.
- Early Irish priests, monks, and nuns were married, often to each other.

- Early monasteries were single gender.
- Early monasteries had both a male and a female side.

- Monasteries had an abbot/abbess who served as leader of the community.
- The Irish Christians did not believe in hierarchy within the Church.

- Early Irish monasteries were remote clusters of hermit monks.
- Early Irish monasteries were social and cultural centers that functioned as universities and taught students from all over the world.

Typical of the Irish love for contradictions, all of these are true. To understand Irish Christianity we will examine some historical examples of these dichotomies, but it is also interesting to note that for those of us who grew up in strong Catholic parishes run by priests, with Catholic schools staffed by nuns, these ancient Christian models were clearly reflected in our American Catholic childhoods.

To understand how these contradictions can all be true, you need to know that early Irish monastic Christianity came in three forms, just as so many historical and mythological Irish elements do. They were:

1. Community monasticism
2. Green/white martyrdom monasticism
3. Peregrination monasticism

Community Monasticism

You will remember that the Irish people lived in raths, circular villages surrounded by circular ditches and filled with (mostly) circular huts. Ireland did not have large cities. The Romans organized their world in large, well-governed cities. Although Rome surely

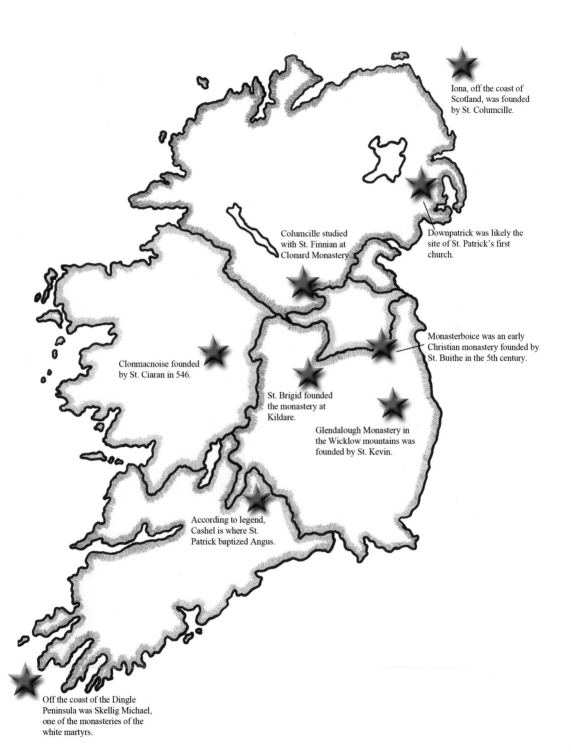

Iona, off the coast of Scotland, was founded by St. Columcille.

Downpatrick was likely the site of St. Patrick's first church.

Columcille studied with St. Finnian at Clonard Monastery.

Monasterboice was an early Christian monastery founded by St. Buithe in the 5th century.

Clonmacnoise founded by St. Ciaran in 546.

St. Brigid founded the monastery at Kildare.

Glendalough Monastery in the Wicklow mountains was founded by St. Kevin.

According to legend, Cashel is where St. Patrick baptized Angus.

Off the coast of the Dingle Peninsula was Skellig Michael, one of the monasteries of the white martyrs.

wanted the Irish Christian world to follow the Roman model, the Irish, as they have always done, went their own way with the new religion. That way was based, structurally and socially, upon the Irish rath, whose structure lent itself perfectly to monasteries. Those monasteries eventually became the first universities of Ireland and later the first universities of Europe.

For a truly thorough understanding of this history, you must read Thomas Cahill's *How the Irish Saved Civilization.* To immerse yourself in a fictional world of Irish monastic life, you should read Peter Tremayne's (Celtic scholar Peter Berresford Ellis's pseudonym) Sister Fidelma mystery series. Both will allow you to vicariously experience the world of Irish monasticism, which must have been a brilliant world indeed.

Early Irish monasteries had a church, of course. They had "cells" or quarters for the monk or nuns or both. Eventually they had students; in fact, prominent families from all over Ireland and Europe sent their children to study in these great monasteries. Students and their teachers needed living space. They needed food, so the monastery had refectories, gardens, herb gardens, and people to tend those. Of course, sometimes people get sick, so they needed apothecaries and physicians. Lawyers were required to adjudicate disputes and rule on the law. Pilgrims came to visit the monastery so they needed guest quarters. Sometimes the monks had to ride out into the countryside or go to a council at another monastery, so they needed horses or mules. Those require stables and blacksmiths. Pretty soon, you have a whole community of people working together for similar purposes.

Because marriage was not forbidden in the Irish Church and because the position of women in Ireland was different from that of women in Rome, whole monastic communities were founded and organized by Christian women. In other communities, both men and women taught and lived in gender-based "wings" of the monastery.

In Tremayne's Sister Fidelma series, Fidelma is a nun—and she is a lawyer—and she is married to her soulmate, a monk named Brother Eadulf. All of this is representative of the monastic Irish model.

St. Brigid of Kildare

You will remember from the first part of our book that an ancient goddess named Brighid, part of the Brighid/Anu/Dana trinity, was an important part of pre-Christian Irish life. However, there is also a St. Brigid, who founded her own monastery and school in Kildare, Ireland. Born around 451 A.D., she was the daughter of Dubhtach, one of the great chiefs from Leinster. Her mother was evidently a slave. Although there is enough historical evidence to suggest that St. Brigid actually existed, in typical Irish fashion, legends about her abound. One says that she gave away all her father's wealth—and even his sword—to the poor. Several say that she healed lepers, and one particularly graphic legend says that she poked out her own eye so that she wouldn't have to marry and could keep her commitment to Christ. One of the most interesting and persistent legends was that the location of Brigid's monastery had been a pagan shrine where a perpetual fire burned, and she and her sisters tended it.

It is likely that she founded the monastery at Kildare (*Cill Dara*, in Irish) in the fifth century. She established it as a two-sided monastery, i.e., one that included abbots and abbesses, nuns and brothers, and students of both genders. She also founded an art school where, supposedly, a gorgeous illustrated version of the gospels was produced. Her monastery was likely the closest representation of our childhood parish schools in America, a subject that we will return to later.

The fascinating *Annals of Kildare* (from which one could write a hundred novels) record a list of the abbesses of Kildare that runs from St. Brigid all the way up to the year 1171, after both the Viking and the Norman invasions! On it are such interesting names as Affraic, Eithne (Irish name of the folk singer Enya), Gormlaith, and Muireann (akin to the modern Maureen). Evidently these abbesses were so powerful that family members "inherited" the title in some generations, while wars were fought to install women from certain influential families into the position in other periods of history. Sidebar stories in the *Annals* tell us of Viking invasions (more on that later) and even of a queen who discovered a plot against her husband while she was having the church rebuilt.

Whether St. Brigid wrote the poem below or not, it typifies the hospitality of the Irish monastic system and the complete lack of separation in the Irish Christian mind between heavenly things and earthly things. There are dozens of different translations of this poem, but here is its essence. As you read it, imagine what it would have been like to dwell in an early Christian community of such hospitality, gratitude, and joy.

St. Brigid and the Lake of Beer, by Brother Mickey McGrath, OSFS. (Used with permission of Michael O'Neill McGrath/bromickeymcgrath.com.) The painting is based upon a joyous poem supposedly written by St. Brigid herself.

I should like a lake of beer for the King of Kings.
I should like the angels of heaven to be tippling there for all of time.
I should like the men of heaven to live with me, to sing and dance.
White cups of love I would give them, with a full heart.
Sweet pitchers of mercy I would give to every man.
I would make heaven a cheerful place for the happy heart is true
and men should be contented, for their own sake
and for Christ, whom I pray loves me too.
I would gather the people from all of the parishes
and give special welcome to the women,
to the three Marys of great renown.
I would sit by the lake of beer with the men and women of God
and we would toast for all eternity.

Martyrs Green and White

The monastic model was not the only model for Christianity in early Ireland. Another form emerged that was as remote and difficult as any lifestyle choice in the history of the world. The so-called green and white martyrs were Christians who decided that the best way to honor their commitment to Christianity was to do it either all alone in a remote location or in a community of men in a remote location. Some scholars say that the impulse to remove themselves from all that they loved—family, friends, food, feasts, beer, and mead—arose because these monks felt either deprived of having or guilty for not having had the martyrdom experience of Roman Christians. So, they denied themselves everything human and warm in order to suffer like their Continental brothers and sisters.

This theory, however, does not explain the impulse to go into exile

The lake at Glendalough.

with a community. Nor does it take into account a basic characteristic of the Irish from time immemorial, and that is that Irish sociability vies with a need to be alone and undisturbed in the quiet contemplation of nature. Remember that to our ancient ancestors, nature itself was mystical, imbued with spirit, the physical manifestation of the Maker, if you will. Perhaps the impulse of the green martyrs was toward what Catholic philosopher and theologian John O'Donohue points out in *Anam Cara,* his seminal work on Celtic Christianity. Our ancient Irish ancestors knew, with certainty, that the "silence of landscape conceals vast presence."

Whatever their reasons, off they went.

Remember that St. Kevin took himself all alone to the two lakes at Glendalough and lived in a cave, surrounded by only light and wind, birds and fish, and a wondrous bowl of sky reflected in the water below. He didn't want followers; he wanted to be alone in the company of God. He managed to pull it off for seven years, but then followers found him and set up an encampment. The monastic city described above began to grow around him, making him a white martyr.

Why did they follow him? Well, as John O'Donohue tells us, there is "unprecedented spiritual hunger in our times." There was in the time of the white martyrs also; that may be true of every time.

Perhaps followers who cannot feed that spiritual hunger with their own prayer or solitude seek out someone who has done so, believing that he, or she, possesses the secret—the answer to the loneliness and longing that constitute the human condition.

Whatever the reason, some of the white martyrs got very creative in their attempts to get away from any potential followers. Some took themselves to remote locations and lived alone in little stone clochans that must have been similar to St. Patrick's dwelling as a slave.

Monastic stone clochan on the Dingle Peninsula in the south of Ireland.

Others abandoned Ireland completely. One group of monks rowed offshore to the skelligs, a cluster of remote and unwelcoming rocks south of Ireland in the heaving sea. Here, on Skellig Michael (*Sceilig Mhichíl,* in Irish), they set up an entire monastery of clochans in the clattering rain and changeable sea-wind, high on a promontory and ten miles offshore. This self-exile could hardly have been called green—grey might have been a better appellation. Nonetheless, they lasted there from the sixth century to the ninth when they were attacked by Vikings, but even then the monks returned and continued their difficult lifestyle. They did not abandon the island until the twelfth century when, evidently deciding they were at the end of their exile, they moved back to the mainland.

How they gardened or ate or bore the constant howl and damp is beyond our modern comprehension, but they did so generation after generation.

Columcille the Peregrinator

A third type of monastic brotherhood functioned much more like ancient Irish bards; off they went like migrating birds to found monasteries all over Europe, carrying their knowledge with them. One of the most interesting of these wandering monks was Colum of Donegal, who eventually became known as St. Columcille (Colum of the Church, pronounced *Cawl-um-kill,* because the Irish *c* is hard) and/or St. Columba. He ended up founding more than thirty monasteries, but the most interesting, on the island of Iona off the coast of Scotland, eventually gave rise to the Book of Kells, an unusual development indeed when you consider that Columcille went to Iona for the first violation of copyright in history!

Like many of the saints of Ireland, Colum does not come down to us as a quiet and holy man of peace. He was a warrior from a warrior family—great-great-grandson of the same Niall of the Nine Hostages who captured St. Patrick into slavery. We could also rightly say that he had an obsession with learning, books, and biblical knowledge.

One of the greatest teachers of Colum's time was a priest named Finnian, who presided over Clonard Monastery (see the earlier map of monasteries). He was evidently so extraordinary that the monastery boasted over three thousand students! At some point later in his life, Colum asked Finnian if he could borrow Finnian's psalter, a handwritten copy of the psalms. Finnian agreed, but Colum went behind his back and copied the book by hand. According to legend, light streamed from Columcille's fingers while he was at this task in the dark church. Finnian was furious, so furious that he took the case to trial before the Ard Ri of Tara, Diarmaid Mac Cerbhaill, the high king of Ireland. The king ruled in Finnian's favor, saying, "To every cow its calf, to every book its copy." Any American author will tell you that this is a highly relevant argument in the digital age, but it was evidently a hot subject in the sixth century as well. Additionally, it fed into a feud between the northern Ui Neill clan and the southern Ui Neill, of whom the high king was a member. The long and short of it is that eventually it resulted in the great Battle of Cul Dreimhne, in which 3,000 Ui Neill men were slaughtered.

History tells us variously that Columcille either fought in this battle or prayed for victory in this battle and afterward felt so guilt-ridden for his part in the deaths that he exiled himself to Iona, never to return. Supposedly the *Cathac of St. Columba* in the National Museum of Ireland is the very book over which a war broke out.

Whether any of this is true or not, Columcille did found a great monastic university on the island of Iona where he taught and converted the Picts of Scotland and the Dal Riata Irish who had moved to Scotland years before. Perhaps more importantly, it was Columcille and his monks who illustrated the Book of Kells, the gorgeous illustrated version of the gospels that is housed in the Trinity College Library, Dublin. We will discuss the history of that book later in this chapter.

Some legends say that Columcille's body was returned to Ireland after his death, while others say that he returned once during his lifetime for a Church conference, but did so blindfolded so as not to break his vow of exile. Whatever the true story, waves of monks were to follow his example, founding monasteries all over Europe. As an odd side note, they almost always traveled as a group of twelve—eleven monks and their abbot—in imitation of the twelve apostles.

Estimates are that the Irish founded more than 150 European monasteries, all told!

European Monasteries Founded by Irish Monks

- St. Columbanus founded Luxeuil Abbey in Luxeuil–les-Bains, France, in the late sixth century on the site of what had once been a mixed Roman/Gallic town called Luxovium. Evidently Columbanus, like so many Irish saints, had a temper and a quick tongue, which eventually got him banished from this monastery by the French king. A fascinating fact about this abbey was that it had so many choirs that *laus perennis,* or "unceasing praise" or song, continued on a twenty-four-hour schedule.
- St. Trudpert trudged all the way to the Black Forest in Germany to found a monastery that is now home to an order of nuns.
- St. Killian, from County Cavan, founded a monastery in Wurzburg, Germany, but in a "Hamletesque" twist, he was murdered by the wife of the duke. She had been the widow of the duke's brother, and Killian advised the duke that such a marriage was not acceptable in Catholic law at the time. Hell hath no fury. . . .
- St. Gall, disciple of St. Columbanus, founded a green martyr's hermitage in Switzerland and refused to be bishop or abbot so that he could remain a hermit. After his death, St. Othmar created a community monastery and named it after the hermit.
- Bobbio was founded by St. Columbanus in the seventh century north of Genoa in Italy. Known for the finest library in all of Italy, the abbey there was the site for Umberto Eco's novel *The Name of the Rose.* One art scholar claims that Bobbio is the scenic backdrop for Da Vinci's *Mona Lisa.*

The Magnificent Book of Kells

Try to imagine this: it is sometime in the eighth century. You are a monk, hunched in the scriptorium of a monastery on the island of Iona; St. Columcille (Columba) is your founder. Your brothers call you Caiside—the Curly-Haired.

Outside it is raining and the salt smell of the sea is strong. The persistent damp has chilled your bones. You are dipping your quill in gall—a purple-brown ink made from oak and salt.

The room is dark. Your abbot has provisioned it with fat tallow candles on tall iron stands and smaller tabletop candles of beeswax. He has seen to it that a fire burns constantly, but you are building the complex swirls and knotwork of a letter from the Gospel of John and you squint against the wet light.

Nearby, Brother Eamon is coloring the Virgin's gown. He uses the rich blue color ground from lapis lazuli brought from the farthest reaches of Persia. He hums while he works. You envy him his calm.

None of you can hurry this intricate work, and yet you know that you must. Lochlanders from the North have been harrying the coastal monasteries. They do not know the name of the one true God, but gold and silver—that they know. This book, this glorious praise of the Almighty, cannot fall into their hands.

And so you pull the beeswax candle closer, arch your body over the calf vellum, and delicately, delicately, bring the word of God onto the page.

The Chi Rho page from the Book of Kells. (Image used here by licensing arrangement with Art Resource Fine Art Licensing, New York, USA)

The Book of Kells is glorious beyond description. Comprising illustrated, handwritten versions of the four gospels, it is so detailed that close study reveals layers and layers of complexity. It must indeed reflect the monastic sense of God—abundant, intricate, celebratory, beautiful, colorful, whimsical, arcane—in the truest Celtic sense.

It resides in the library of Trinity College in Dublin (whose upstairs room was George Lucas's inspiration for the Jedi Library in the *Star Wars* trilogy). Through a glass tabletop, you can gaze down upon the book, not quite the size of a present-day hardback, and marvel at its Lilliputian world. In order to make the modern mind understand its complexity, the room that contains it also holds huge lighted murals of the book's pages in which birds curl back upon themselves, single letters of the alphabet reveal carpets of flowers, and the elfin faces of tiny people peer up from the margins. The endless knotwork proclaims the continuous Irish message that life flows into life; there is no death.

Kells was probably begun on the island of Iona—at least that seems to be the most widely accepted theory. At some point, due to Viking "visitors," the monks had to flee with it, evidently to the inland monastery of Kells, where it remained for centuries. Kells is not the only illustrated version of the gospels, but it is certainly the most famous. If you want to view a whimsical documentary of the illustration and protection of the book, watch the artistically exquisite animated film *Secret of Kells.*

Other Illustrated Books of the Bible

- *The Cathac of St. Columba. Cathac* means, literally, "militant," a name the book received after Columcille fought on behalf of the northern Ui Neill.
- *The Book of Durrow.* No one knows quite where this book was illustrated, but it was certainly part of Columcille's training school in illuminated gospels (he never did get over his obsession with books).
- *The Lindisfarne Gospels.* These were illustrated in Northumbria by a single artistic monk named Eadfrith; it's very rare that a single illustrator made one of these books.
- *The Book of Kildare.* This book has vanished, and some scholars conflate it with the Book of Kells.

How to Illustrate the Gospels from the Bible

- Begin with vellum (calfskin) or parchment (sheepskin). Remove all debris, then cure it with lime. Stretch it on a frame, smooth it with a pumice stone, then cut it to a page shape.
- Make your pens from sharpened goose quills and your ink from iron gall, a mixture of oak stain, iron salt, and water.
- Mix your colors: yellow from ochre; red from lead; blue from indigo or ground lapis lazuli imported from the Middle East, if your monastery has money; purple from lichens; green from verdigris lifted from metals. In some cases you can also melt gold, though the Book of Kells does not use gold leaf.

- Now put your scribes to work on the words, under the tutelage and watchful eyes of the scriptorium master. Have them work in natural light as much as possible, as blindness is a risk with this work.
- Now set your artists free, knowing full well that they may spend weeks on a single page. The heads of dragons will weave around the tiniest of smiling human faces. Braids of flowers over and under words and intricate knotwork will indicate that life flows into and out of life—there is no death. The gospels will now be the physical symbol of that hope, written, preserved, and preaching hope and joy on each breathtaking page.
- Create a book coffin, a golden box encrusted with jewels and still more braidwork. Here you will preserve, and hopefully protect, your book.
- Create a place in the monastery to hide the precious book in its box, and pray that the Northmen never find it and destroy it.

St. Brendan's Magical Mystery Tour

Of all the peregrinations of our monastic monks, none is stranger or more fascinating than the *Navigatio* of St. Brendan the Navigator, a story filled with wonder and driven by unparalleled Irish wanderlust. But before we travel where no other monks had gone before, we need to meet St. Brendan, because, like all of our own ancestors, he was willing to journey far, far from home, filled with hope and wonder.

Brendan was born in County Kerry, in the south of Ireland, at the end of the fifth century. He studied at the monastery of St. Ita, another one of the great abbesses of Ireland. Then, in the great tradition of our white martyrs, he founded monastery after monastery, wandering all over the Celtic fringe and setting up houses from Galway (Clonfert Monastery) to the Aran Islands and even over to the Brittany coast of France. Obviously, Brendan came honestly to his seafaring wanderlust.

The story of his astonishing voyage was written down in the tenth century, and Brendan supposedly died around 577 A.D. at the age of ninety-three! That may be proof that sea air is good for us but not necessarily that his voyage actually took place or that it went to all the locations it purported to go. There is no better story, however, for Brendan's voyage is *Star Trek, Close Encounters of the Third Kind,* and *E.T.,* all rolled into one.

The Dingle Peninsula of Ireland.

A relative of Niall of the Nine Hostages (our Niall got around, didn't he?) came to St. Brendan and told him a wild story of sailing to the Land of Promise. Based on this vagary, Brendan decided to leave his monastery and glide away. He chose fourteen monks, fasted for forty days, and departed, evidently from somewhere on the Dingle Peninsula.

Brendan's craft was a currach, an ancient type of Irish boat made of wicker and covered with a cowhide salved in (of all things) butter. Brendan put sails on this questionably seaworthy vessel, and he and the brothers took off, headed north into the cold, open sea.

From that point on, the voyage becomes fantastical. The brothers find an island inhabited only by a dog and a mansion full of food, an island of pure white sheep, and a paradise of birds, one of whom flies to them with tinkling bells on its wings and speaks to them in their own language. Later, after they have been lost at sea for forty days, they come to an island full of ancient monks, who feed them. Sea monsters, evidently great whales, swim up beside and around them, and at one point, the brothers circle back and end up at an island they have visited before. One day, a bird brings them grapes and they find an island with vineyards. Most fantastical of all, they are attacked by a dragon, encounter a huge column of some marble material in the middle of the sea, and sail past an island that seems to be the furnace of hell. At last they reach an "autumn land" rich with fruits and divided by a river whose opposite bank is Paradise. The voyage takes seven years, but amazingly, the monks return safely to Ireland.

Whether the fantastical nature of the voyage is true or not, the voyage itself was possible. How do we know? Because in 1976, adventurer, historian, and medalist of the Royal Geographic Society Tim Severin duplicated the voyage exactly, using the same type of boat constructed with the same methods. He concluded that not only could the voyage have taken place exactly as the legend tells it but that it is likely that the locations it describes are the Hebrides, Iceland, and Newfoundland in the New World! This hearkens back to our first chapter, in which we theorized that our Irish ancestors came to our shores long before Columbus. If you have never read Severin's book, it is an adventure of the first order and does St. Brendan proud for the wild and frightening elements of the modern journey and their echoes of the ancient legend.

How Irish Christianity Became Roman Christianity

By now you have surmised that our ancestors' form of Christianity was far different from the form we grew up with. It was communal or it wandered the world. It was rooted in the sense that all of creation was sacred. It was not very hierarchical. It was not sexist. It was deeply and constantly mystical.

Still other things were different about the Irish Church, some of them seemingly small, but not to the Roman Church. The Irish did not confess to a father confessor. Instead, they confessed to an anam cara, a beloved soul, a dear and trusted friend to whom they told their failings. This friend then advised them on how to right any wrongs. (St. Patrick gets very upset in his journal about the fact that he told his anam cara a secret sin from his youth and the anam cara ratted him out to the bishops in France, an absolute violation of his trust.)

The Irish men tonsured their hair in the old druidic fashion. They drew a line across their head from ear to ear, shaved everything in front of the line, and let the back grow long. Rome wanted circular tonsures in the center of the head.

Of major importance to Rome were the issues of celibacy and the date of Easter. Rome wanted Easter to be calculated by the rules set down in 325 at the Council of Nicaea, while the Irish were still calculating it by older methods.

Now, in point of fact, the argument wasn't really about tonsures and Easter dates. It was, as always, about power. In 664 A.D., the Church called a synod or council at Whitby Abbey on the coast of England. This was a double abbey presided over by an amazing abbess named Hilda or Hild (read Nicola Griffith's superb fictional biography, entitled *Hild*). Hilda favored the Celtic rules, but under tremendous pressure both politically and from his wife, who was Roman Catholic, King Oswy of Northumbria ruled in favor of Rome.

This decision caused the Irish and Scots monasteries to do what our ancestors (and maybe our own family members) always do— stubbornly push on with their own tried-and-true ways for as long as they could. But eventually, the Irish monasteries on the Continent became more and more Roman, and at last, the monasteries in Scotland and Ireland did as well.

You could rightly say that the Catholic Church of our American-Irish childhoods was determined in a windy, cliff-side abbey in the year 664 A.D.

8

Gone Viking

Scholars are very divided about the uses of round towers in Ireland. Traditionally they believed that the high doors and high vantage point were employed to spot Vikings and then to hide the monks far above the ground during attacks. Now, however, many disagree with that assessment and say that they were simply bell towers.

On the second floor of the National Museum of Ireland on Kildare Street in Dublin, you can meet a Viking. He is dead, of course, but spend some time with him and your imagination will re-flesh the long, thick bones. He was a tall fellow, well over six feet. Likely he had a thick head of red or gold hair, a long, bushy moustache, and a mighty hand with a blade.

It is completely appropriate that he is there in Dublin because Dubh Linn, the Dark Pool behind what is now Dublin Castle, became, at one point, a Viking neighborhood, but that population shift took a while to occur. Meanwhile, the beginning of the Viking invasions predicted the end of the Golden Monastic Age of Ireland.

The Vikings—meaning pirates or sea wanderers—began to invade Ireland in the late eighth century. The predominant raiders were from Norway and were called Lochlanders or Lochlainn; the Danes were known as Danair. For a very long time, they raided coastal monasteries only (you will remember that they raided the monks on Skellig Michael). They plundered everything and took it back to Norway—

cattle, golden book covers, chalices, communion plates—everything that wasn't bolted down. Men, women, and children—even monks from the monasteries they raided—were sent back as slaves called thralls.

Eventually they also began to raid inland. Their longboats had flat hulls with little draw; this allowed them to move silently and far up the rivers of Ireland, gathering still more plunder. In 1006, at the monastery of Kells, both the book and the golden shrine in which it was kept were stolen, likely by Vikings. The book shrine has never reappeared but the book itself was found in a ditch covered by sod.

Perhaps it was the warmer weather or perhaps the fertile land, but eventually the Vikings began to settle in. They founded the towns now known as Limerick and Dublin, among others. In the 1970s the ruins of a complete ninth-century Viking settlement were found in the area of Wood Quay in Dublin, but Dublin City Council offices now rest atop the site. Although protests against this spectacular archeological sacrilege

were held in Dublin, corporate and bureaucratic forces won the battle; the artifacts from the dig were moved to the National Museum.

The fact that there was an entire Viking town there indicates how much the Vikings became part of the fabric of Ireland. They traded, sometimes fought with and sometimes against local Irish chiefs, and carried on a massive slave market in Dublin. First Norse and later Danish Vikings spent more than two hundred years attacking Ireland, setting up port cities and plundering far and wide. DNA studies are ongoing to determine just how much of the Irish gene pool is Viking.

Eventually, once the Vikings settled permanently, the Irish chiefs began to band together to eliminate them. But their demise did not come until 1014, under the great chief Brian Boru.

Brian Boru: Irish King Defeats the Vikings

For Irish-Americans, it is interesting to note that it is very likely that both Pres. Ronald Reagan and Pres. John F. Kennedy were related down the long ancestral pipe to Brian Boru, one of the greatest warrior chiefs in Irish history.

Brian Boru was born Brian Bóruma Mac Cennétig, his father's name

(Library of Congress Digital Collection)

(Library of Congress Digital Collection)

The Rock of Cashel, stronghold of Brian Boru and site of his crowning as king.

being an early Irish form of "Kennedy." When he was quite young, he fought beside his brother Mathgamain and helped him to defeat the Vikings of Limerick, but when the Vikings killed Mathgamain in 976, Brian took vengeance and killed the Viking king Ivor.

Brian's long history is complex. The Irish kings sometimes united against the Vikings or fought against each other, but Brian became one of the icons of Irish history when he and his son Murchad defeated the Vikings in the Battle of Clontarf, fought on Good Friday in 1014. Both Murchad and Brian were killed, Brian being cut to ribbons in his battle tent by retreating Vikings.

To really understand Brian's colorful and complex history, read Morgan Llywelyn's *Lion of Ireland.*

With the advent of the Vikings, the quiet, artistic life of monastic Christianity was forever changed. It would not be the last time that religious life in Ireland was disturbed by invaders. The British under Queen Elizabeth I and later Oliver Cromwell were profoundly destructive to Irish Catholicism, and the cataclysm known as the Great Famine influenced Catholicism not only in Ireland but here in America, as we will see in the next chapters.

For Further Reading: An Annotated Bibliography

Nonfiction

Bamford, Christopher, and William Parker Marsh. *Celtic Christianity: Ecology and Holiness.* Aurora, CO: Lindisfarne Press, 1982.
   This lovely little book is full of Celtic Christian prayers, stories, and hymns.

Barnes, Ian. *The Historical Atlas of the Celtic World.* New York: Chartwell Books, 2011.
   Its superb maps of monastic settlements and Viking invasions are relevant for this chapter.

Brown, Peter. *The Book of Kells.* London: Thames & Hudson, 1980.
   Gorgeous illustrations from the Book of Kells are accompanied by good explanations of how the book was created.

Cahill, Thomas. *How the Irish Saved Civilization: The Untold Story of Ireland's Heroic Role from the Fall of Rome to the Rise of Medieval Europe.* New York: Doubleday, 1995.
   This is the granddaddy of all studies on Irish monasticism. It looks at the temper of Celtic Christianity, at the monastic impulse to voyage, and at the results of a plague- and barbarian-devastated Europe. If you love the study of Irish Christianity, you will read this book again and again.

Constable, Nick. *Ancient Ireland.* London: Kiln House, 1996.
   Gorgeous photographs of pre-Christian and early Christian sites are featured here.

De Paor, Liam. *The Peoples of Ireland: From Prehistory to Modern Times.*
    Notre Dame, IN: University of Notre Dame Press, 1986.
    De Paor looks at pre-Christian and early Christian Ireland, then focuses
on the centuries of invasions and their effects upon indigenous culture.

——. *Saint Patrick's World.* Dublin: Four Courts Press, 1993.
    A clear and well-organized introduction is followed by lots of
documents from the period.

Duffy, Joseph. *Patrick in His Own Words.* Dublin: Veritas, 2000.
    A translation of Patrick's Confession and Letter to Coroticus is
followed by explanations and context for each.

Duncan, Anthony. *The Elements of Celtic Christianity.* Boston: Element
    Books, 1992.
    This little book is a treasure trove because it clearly articulates the
character of Celtic Christianity and delineates the differences between
Celtic and Roman Christianity.

Freeman, Mara. *Kindling the Celtic Spirit.* San Francisco: HarperCollins,
    2000.
    Freeman is a modern druid practitioner and this book is a lovely study
of Celtic and Druidic customs throughout ancient and modern times.

Freeman, Philip. *St. Patrick of Ireland: A Biography.* New York: Simon
    and Schuster, 2005.
    Freeman's well-organized book provides clear translations of the
Confession and Letter.

Gallico, Paul. *The Steadfast Man: A Biography of St. Patrick.* New York:
    Doubleday, 1958.
    Gallico is a novelist and storyteller (*Too Many Ghosts, The Snow
Goose)* and the result is that this biography seems to grasp the
emotional nuances of Patrick's character.

Green, Miranda J. *The World of the Druids.* London: Thames & Hudson, 1997.
    If you can only own one book on the druids, select this book. It
is wonderfully organized and lavishly illustrated; clearly articulates
what we actually do know about ancient druidic practice, separating

it from myth and speculation by Roman historians; and differentiates it from the reconstructed practices of modern druidic imitators.

Howlett, D. R., trans. and ed. *The Confession of Saint Patrick*. Liguori, MO: Liguori, 1994.

Lehane, Brendan. *Early Celtic Christianity*. New York: Barnes & Noble Books, 1993.
Originally published as *Quest for Three Abbots*, this looks at paganism, early Christianity, and monastic life.

Llywelyn, Morgan. *1014: Brian Boru and the Battle for Ireland*. Dublin: O'Brien Press, 2014.
Morgan Llywelyn's scholarly history of Brian Boru has received great reviews.

McCaffrey, Carmel, and Leo Eaton. *In Search of Ancient Ireland: The Origins of the Irish from Neolithic Times to the Coming of the English*. Chicago: New Amsterdam Books, 2002.
McCaffrey and Eaton take us through the pagan/Christian shift and address the effects of the Vikings on early Irish Christianity.

Moorhouse, Geoffrey. *Sun Dancing: A Vision of Medieval Ireland*. New York: Harcourt Brace, 1997.
Sun Dancing has a very unusual and enjoyable structure, as the first part reads like a novel of early Christianity and the second part presents evidence regarding Finian, Patrick, Brendan, monastic life in Ireland, and more.

O'Donohue, John. *Anam Cara: A Book of Celtic Wisdom*. New York: HarperCollins, 1997.
If you only read one book of Celtic philosophy and theology in your life, it should be this one. O'Donohue, a Celtic Catholic scholar and former Catholic priest, articulates perfectly the ways in which Celtic Christians perceive God and God's created world. To read this book is to be in perfect harmony with our Celtic Christian ancestors.

——. *Eternal Echoes: Celtic Reflections on Our Yearning to Belong*. New York: HarperCollins, 1999.

The Celtic scholar gives his take on loneliness, longing, belonging, and the ways in which they are made more difficult by modern technological life.

Pennick, Nigel. *Celtic Sacred Landscapes.* New York: Thames & Hudson, 1996.
Pennick's book that examines the sacred in the Celtic world from a geographical point of view, focusing on water, hills, stones, rivers, etc. It concludes with an excellent appendix of both pagan and Christian sacred sites.

Ross, Anne, and Don Robins. *The Life and Death of a Druid Prince.* New York: Simon and Schuster, 1989.
This fascinating book examines the ritual killing of an ancient Celt and assesses Celtic sacrificial culture on the basis of the evidence.

Roy, James Charles. *The Road Wet, the Wind Close: Celtic Ireland.* Chester Springs, PA: Dufour Editions, 1986.
Roy's lovely, poetic book perambulates through Celtic and early Christian Ireland and asks questions about the mindsets of both. It is illustrated with moody black-and-white photographs and surely possesses the loveliest title of any book in this list.

Rutherford, Ward. *Celtic Lore: The History of the Druids and Their Timeless Traditions.* London: Aquarian/Thorsons, 1993.
This is a study of druidic traditions and their demise at the hands of Rome.

Scherman, Katharine. *The Flowering of Ireland: Saints, Scholars, and Kings.* New York: Little, Brown, 1981.
Scherman's retellings of the delightfully exaggerated legends surrounding the saints are wonderful and she follows them with scholarly analysis of Christianity's spread through Ireland.

Sellner, Edward C. *Wisdom of the Celtic Saints.* Notre Dame, IN: Ave Maria Press, 1993.
Sellner gives us a wonderfully informative and well-organized source on monastic sites and of stories and sayings from the lives of all of the early Celtic saints.

Severin, Tim. *The Brendan Voyage.* Introduction by Malachy McCourt. New York: Modern Library, 2000.
A hide boat, curious whales, tears in the fabric of the hull, and great sails adorned with Celtic crosses make for an astonishing adventure as Tim Severin and his crew duplicate the magical, legendary voyage of St. Brendan.

Simms, George Otto. *Exploring the Book of Kells.* Dublin: O'Brien Press, 2004.
Simple language and sketches illustrate the history and methods of the Book of Kells.

Sjoestedt, Marie-Louise. *Gods and Heroes of the Celts.* Translated by Myles Dillon. Berkeley, CA: Turtle Island Foundation, 1982.
This is a little book by a great French scholar that nonetheless clearly discusses the gods, mythologies, and mindset of our ancient Celtic forebears.

Skinner, John, trans. *The Confession of Saint Patrick.* New York: Doubleday, 1998.

Snyder, Graydon F. *Irish Jesus, Roman Jesus: The Formation of Early Irish Christianity.* Harrisburg, PA: Trinity Press International, 2002.
Snyder not only shows how the Celtic perception of Christ and Christianity differed from that of Rome but explains why it turned out that way.

Stewart, R. J. *Celtic Gods Celtic Goddesses.* London: Blandford Press, 1990.
This study of the entire panoply of the Irish, Welsh, and Briton gods is beautifully illustrated by Miranda Gray and Courtney Davis.

Van de Weyer, Robert, ed. *Celtic Fire: The Passionate Religious Vision of Ancient Britain and Ireland.* New York: Doubleday, 1990.
Van de Weyer discusses the deep passion of Celtic Christianity and differentiates it from the organizational forms of Roman Christianity.

Wilde, Lyn Webster. *Celtic Women in Legend, Myth and History.* London: Cassell, 1997.

This book includes a superb section on Brigid.

Wood, Juliette. *The Celts: Life, Myth and Art.* New York: Stewart, Tabori and Chang, 1998.
Wood's beautifully illustrated coffee-table book will give you a good visual sense of the complexity and beauty of early Irish Christian art forms.

Fiction

Godwin, Parke. *The Last Rainbow.* New York: Avon Books, 1995.
The intersection of Christianity through the person of St. Patrick with the world of fairies is explored here. The pagan/Christian shift is more of a blend in this novel.

Holland, Cecilia. *The Kings in Winter.* New York: Forge, 1967.
Set during the Viking occupation of Ireland, this historical story of a feud between Brian Boru and another Irish king is told through the eyes of a fictional Irish chieftain. Holland's writing is very evocative.

Lawhead, Stephen. *Byzantium.* New York: Harper Voyager, 1997.
This novel with Christian and Viking themes follows the life of a fictionalized monk assigned to take the Book of Kells to Constantinople.

——. *Patrick.* New York: HarperCollins, 2004.
Although most of the events in this novel never occurred in the life of St. Patrick, Lawhead here examines St. Patrick's missing years, giving him extraordinary journeys and a wife and child. For Patrick purists, this novel is a stretch, but the action is very exciting.

Llywelyn, Morgan. *Lion of Ireland.* New York: Tor Books, 2002.
Llywelyn's novel focuses on the life, loves, and death of Brian Boru, who defeated the Vikings in eleventh-century Ireland.

Osborne-McKnight, Juilene. *I Am of Irelaunde.* New York: Forge, 2001.
Written by the author of this book, *I Am of Irelaunde* is a novel of the pagan/Christian shift as seen through the eyes of St. Patrick and Osian, son of Fionn Mac Cumhail.

Tremayne, Peter.

The deliciousness of sitting down with a mystery from his Sister Fidelma series is beyond description. Fidelma is a nun, lawyer, brilliant mind, and sister of the king. She lives in the fascinating monastic world of communal Christian Ireland, and Tremayne (the pseudonym for historian Peter Berresford Ellis) does a wonderful job of letting us experience that time period in rich detail. Just one warning: once you start these books, you will need to buy/read/reread all of them.

Windsor, Linda. *The Fires of Gleannmara.* 3 vols. Colorado Springs: Multnomah Books, 2000-2002.

These three novels of romance are set in early Christian Ireland. Beginning in the fifth century with the coming of Christianity, Windsor creates three strong Christian female characters.

Video

Blood of the Vikings and Trail of the Vikings. YouTube series. Directed by Julian Richards. BBC Learning, 2001.

This series examines the history of the Vikings and follows a fascinating DNA study of their genetics in Great Britain.

Saint Patrick: The Man, the Myth. DVD. Directed by Patricia Phillips. A&E Television, 1996.

With good photographs, video, and illustrations, this demythologizes Patrick and places him in historical context.

The Secret of Kells. DVD. Directed by Tomm Moore and Nora Twomey. New York Video and Flatiron Films, 2010.

This Academy Award-nominated animated film is exquisite. It is the story of little Brendan, a child in the monastery of Kells, and his fairy friend, Aisling, who work together to protect Ireland's greatest monastic treasure. The story is a sweet delight, but the artwork is breathtaking and worthy of its lofty subject.

No One Leaves Your Table Hungry
Invasion, Starvation, and Emigration

Part III: No One Leaves Your Table Hungry: Invasion, Starvation, and Emigration

9

Eight Hundred Years of Invasions

We have discussed the Viking invasions that began in the eighth century, and certainly the Vikings had a profound effect upon Irish monastic life as well as Irish politics. However, the Vikings were just the first wave of invasions of Ireland, each with worse consequences than the last. These invasions would ruin the Irish clan system, Church, and economy. Eventually, learning, language, and even freedom would fall to these successive invasions, setting the stage for the devastating Famine that may well have brought your ancestors to America.

In these chapters, we will look at that Famine, its causes, and consequences. We will begin with one of the oddest invasions in the storied history of Ireland—the "invited invasion" of the Anglo-Normans.

Who Were the Normans?

In one of the quirks of history, the Normans of Northern France were descendants of two groups we have encountered before—the Vikings who had conquered France and the Gallic Romans, the offspring of the Celtic tribes of France who had long before been conquered by and then intermarried with the Romans. The third group who contributed to the Norman gene pool were the "barbarians" known as the Franks.

Of course, we Americans know Normandy well because our troops landed there on D-Day in World War II. Nearby England made an attractive target, and indeed the Normans invaded England in 1066 at the Battle of Hastings under William the Conqueror, a set of facts we all remember from our high-school study of world history. However, because of the Viking connection, Normans had actually been linked to England for more than a hundred years before this battle.

It's hard to believe, but the tiny darkened area on this map of France is the kingdom of the Normans, source of England's invasion in 1066, of Ireland's nearly a hundred years later, and of the greatest sea landing of World War II.

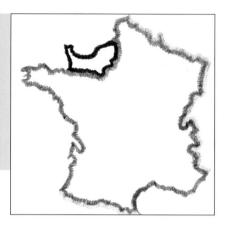

Although some historians say that the Normans only actually ruled England for about a hundred years, the truth is more complex. For example, Elizabeth II, the current queen of England, is the great-(times twenty-two)-granddaughter of William the Conqueror. It is accurate to say that England's culture, language, and customs are largely Norman in origin.

Not so in Ireland, and yet the Normans did indeed invade and conquer Ireland. How that happened is one of the strangest stories in all of Irish history.

The One-Eyed King and the Kidnapped Queen

In the eastern half of Ireland in the twelfth century (more than a hundred years after the defeat of the Vikings), four Irish kings were at war with each other over which one of them should be high king. This was a war of constantly shifting alliances in which each king re-allied himself with others like pieces on a chessboard.

The northernmost chief was Muircheartach MacLochlainn, while the chief of the southeast was Diarmait McMurrough (*Mac Murchada*, in Irish). In the west was Turlough O'Connor.

From our modern perspective, it is nearly impossible to comprehend the shifting sands of these clan wars, but in the midst of these players a one-eyed king named Tiernan O'Rourke (*Tighearnán Mór Ua Ruairc,* in Irish) ruled the kingdom of Breifne. He was married to Dervorgilla (*Derbforgaill,* in Irish), the daughter of the king of Meath. She had been married off to the one-eyed Tiernan O'Rourke at the age of twenty and by all accounts she was a rare beauty.

It is likely that the marriage was one of those clapped-together contract arrangements so popular in the Middle Ages, designed to

MacLochlainn

O'Rourk &
wife Dervorgilla
Kingdom of Breifne

O'Connor

McMurrough

Clan Kings at War
Ireland in 1150

cement political alliances or expand land and holdings. We have no idea if there was any love between Tiernan and Dervorgilla, but in 1152 he was deposed and she was taken into the southeastern kingdom of McMurrough.

Here is where the story gets interesting and strange. While some accounts say that she was kidnapped by McMurrough, the annals of the time show her going off to his kingdom with all of her furniture and cattle. Most abductions do not include the sofa and the cow.

Historians have debated her position for years. Did she love McMurrough? Some sources say she wrote him a letter and asked him to come and get her. Had she been waiting for years for the defeat of her one-eyed husband so that she could go with the man she loved? Or was she taken to the south to keep her safe in the middle of the clan wars, something that her deposed husband could no longer do? Most likely of all, was she a hostage to McMurrough, held to keep her husband in line? Any one of these is a legitimate possibility in those times. The answer would make a fascinating novel because we simply don't know.

Whatever the truth of the matter, after a year, McMurrough turned Dervorgilla over to Turlough O'Connor, chief of the west of Ireland. Evidently she was returned to her husband, Tiernan, for a brief time afterward, but by the year 1154 she was confined, or had confined herself, to the convent at Clonmacnoise. Why? Did none of the men want her now, considering her soiled goods? Or did she long for one man and find herself unable to live with the others? Was she viewed as a Jezebel or traitor? Or did she ask to go to the sisters to be free of the world of feuding kings in which, like her furniture, she was simply moved from one to the other? Perhaps at Clonmacnoise she was allowed some peace and a life of the mind. We can only speculate.

What we do know historically is that Tiernan O'Rourke nursed the emotional wound for years and years, while the political sands around him shifted yet again. In 1166, fourteen years after the "kidnapping," Rory O'Connor (*Ruaidri Ua Conchobair*, in Irish) had become the high king of Ireland. He and Tiernan formed an alliance, defeated Diarmait McMurrough, and took over his castle. Tiernan could have had him executed, but instead he made a fatal mistake. He exiled McMurrough, first forcing him to pay an honor fee of 100 ounces of gold for the "kidnapping" of his wife more than a decade before.

Diarmait McMurrough wanted his kingdom back, so he hied himself over to France, all the way to Aquitaine in the southwest, and asked for help from Henry II, the Norman king of England from the

House of Plantagenet. Henry, for all of us Americans who find British kingship complicated, is the king who caused the death of Thomas a Becket, the archbishop of Canterbury. He was also married to Eleanor of Aquitaine. (If you have never seen the movie *The Lion in Winter*, starring Peter O'Toole and Katharine Hepburn, treat yourself. It is the complex political tale of these two figures, their vast lands, and their very dysfunctional families.)

Henry II allowed McMurrough to collect a Norman army. One year after his exile from Ireland, McMurrough returned with Norman soldiers to get his kingdom back. Here we see the law of unintended consequences gleefully at work, because none of the Irish chiefs, including McMurrough himself, was aware that the Norman invasion of Ireland had already begun.

Ireland fell fast. By 1170, Richard de Clare, earl of Pembroke, a Norman nobleman better known as Strongbow, arrived to "help" McMurrough. The two immediately cemented their alliance by marrying McMurrough's daughter Aoife to Strongbow. No history ever mentions how Aoife felt about being a chess piece in a foreign military alliance, but soon after the marriage, her father died and Strongbow inherited the kingdom of Leinster in Ireland.

Henry II, a little worried about Strongbow's rapid gains, followed in 1171 and forced all the kings of Ireland to swear fealty to him. By 1183, Rory O'Connor, the last Ard Ri (high king) of Ireland, was expelled by his own family and not the Normans (he had arrested several brothers and blinded one to keep the throne). He went into a monastery and Ireland became, for all intents and purposes, a Norman country.

Malahide Castle, north of Dublin, sits on land awarded to the Tailbois (later called Talbot) family of Norman warriors. Tailbois was one of the earliest Norman warriors who came in with Henry II in the twelfth century. The structure of the original castle is classic Norman, and this castle should be a must on any tour of Norman historical sites.

Bunratty Castle, now the site of medieval tourist banquets, was first granted to a Norman lord in 1250 and later to Thomas de Clare, descendant of Strongbow. The current castle is the fourth one on the site and became the stronghold of the O'Briens, the earls of Thomond. It sits at the edge of the Bunratty Folk Park, all of which makes for a lovely, photogenic day trip for Americans who have no idea of the history we are treading on here.

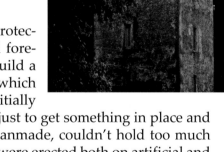

Life in a Norman Keep

The warlike Normans built for protection, so their homes were first and foremost fortresses. They would first build a *motte*, a large manmade hill, atop which they put an observation tower. Initially these towers were wooden, in part just to get something in place and in part because the motte, being manmade, couldn't hold too much weight. But eventually stone keeps were erected both on artificial and natural hills.

Around the keep the Normans created a bailey, an outer court enclosed by a defensive wall. In the bailey, whole cities would grow up. Its wall might have several towers along it, good not only for viewing the surrounding countryside but also for raining down arrows, fire, hot oil, and other tools of war upon attackers. Outside the wall, there might well be a ditch lined with sharpened sticks. These fortifications became the Norman castles of Ireland. Of course, eventually, massive castles with walls, towers, and moats grew up all over Europe.

A keep could be round or a tall, square, stone tower. That was the shape that predominated in Ireland, and eventually "keep" houses sprang up all over, built not only by the Normans but the Irish themselves. Interestingly, the original Norman word for this keep was a *donjon*, obviously the basis for the far creepier term "dungeon." Windsor Castle in England is an example of a motte with two baileys, one on either side of the motte.

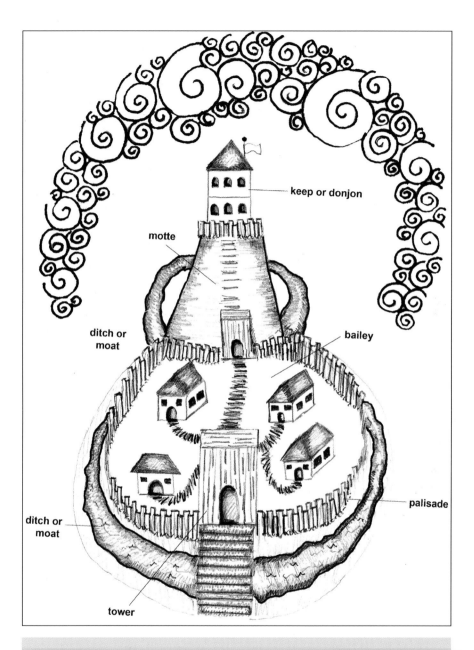

keep or donjon

motte

ditch or moat

bailey

ditch or moat

palisade

tower

The keep was high up on the motte, surrounded by a ditch or moat with a removable raised bridge, sometimes with a murder hole (for hot oil, etc.) overhead. The bailey would contain everything from stables to kitchens.

A Norman keep, as you will see from the cutaway illustration opposite, consisted of three or four floors. It could be forty feet high and the walls were incredibly thick—seven to twenty feet. If there was a floor at the base, it was often sealed shut and could only be entered from inside the castle; there was no outside door. It could be used to store food, weapons, or treasure. Sometimes servants or soldiers also had rooms and barracks on this bottom floor, from which they could rise into the main house, but if the keep had four stories, both knights and servants would live on the second floor.

The Great Hall was reached by a set of spiral stairs; in a four-story keep it would be on the third floor. It would be a large, paneled room with huge trestle tables. Servants could climb the stairs to bring food, and sometimes these great halls had galleries where musicians and singers might entertain. Mass would also be celebrated here every day, because the Normans were Catholic.

Still another floor up would be the living quarters of the lord and his family. For safety, the sleeping rooms were hard to reach and guarded from the floors below.

A garderobe would be somewhere off to the side of this floor and another might be on the banqueting floor. The garderobe was a latrine. A long stone bench with holes in it served as toilet facilities, and waste dropped all the way to the ground level far below. The stench of ammonia was strong in the garderobe, so the family sometimes hung their clothes here in order to kill fleas and lice that might be tempted to infest the clothing that was seldom (if ever) cleaned.

In some keeps, a nursery room led off from the sleeping floor. Access to these nurseries would be by spiral staircases that were constructed to be too narrow for a knight to draw his sword. In fact, spiral staircases throughout the keep were designed to favor the sword arm of the owner and hamper that of any attacker trying to climb the steps.

In the bailey city surrounding the keep were kitchens, slaughter-houses, herb gardens, perhaps a doctor or apothecary, blacksmith facilities, soldiers' quarters, stables, and anything else needed for daily life even in times of war or siege.

Obviously, Norman life was built entirely around war and siege, safety and conquest.

How the Normans Became More Irish Than the Irish

By the early 1300s all of the areas outlined in purple were Anglo-Norman in population but the area controlled by traditional Irish clans had shrunk to the areas indicated in green. However, once England stopped paying attention—or considering the Norman Irish as English—the Irish clans began to attack and reclaim land.

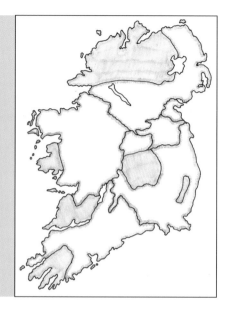

Once the Normans got settled in Ireland, they subsumed their identity into the Irish identity, especially as they moved into the north and west. They married into Irish families and took Irish surnames. They became part of the Irish clan system and began to form alliances with Irish chiefs.

Then, in the thirteenth century, the Irish realized that the Normans no longer had the military backing—or even the attention—of the British crown. Recruiting assistance from the Scots, they began to attack Norman lords and regain their lands.

By the late 1300s, the Normans had been defeated, had departed, or had become so "Gaelic" in their behaviors that they considered themselves Irish. This is when the English crown woke up and became frightened of losing all control in Ireland. King Edward III sent his son Lionel at the head of an army, but when they did not succeed in re-conquering anything, Lionel decided to impose his will upon the Norman Irish simply by saying it was so.

He called a meeting at Kilkenny in 1366 and declared the "Statutes of Kilkenny." While many of his proclamations have to do with theft, law, war, and excommunication, the statutes designed to separate the Anglo-Normans from the Irish are listed below.

No English (Anglo-Norman) person could:
- Marry an Irish person.
- Put children into fosterage with an Irish family.
- Give a child an Irish name.
- Speak the Irish language.
- Play the Irish game of hurling.
- Ride a horse without English clothes and saddles.
- Have any contact with Irish storytellers, poets, or pipers.
- Utilize Irish brehon law for any reason.
- Admit any Irishman to education or holy orders.

Lionel tried to put teeth into the measure by saying that if the Anglo-Normans did not follow these rules, he would seize their lands and all their money, take away their titles, and have them imprisoned. But his statutes were largely ignored.

Ten years later, however, Richard II arrived with an army and did manage to enforce some of the statutes, forcing Anglo-Norman Irish lords to re-swear their loyalty to a king and crown from whom they had been separated for two hundred years. Eventually most of these lords rebelled and took back their Irish lands.

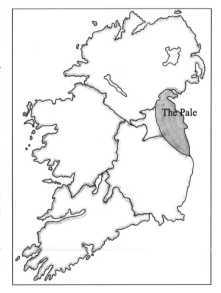

By 1450, the last true Anglo-Norman part of Ireland was reduced to an area around Dublin known as the Pale. Here lived the last vestiges of Anglo-Normans loyal to England. That tiny strip is shown on this map in purple.

It might have seemed that the Irish had defeated another enemy—this time by simply absorbing them—and they could go back to the original clan system of ancient Ireland. But the truth was that England was biding its time and that a far worse curse than the Normans would arrive in Ireland a hundred years hence in the form of the Tudors of England.

Meanwhile, for our purposes as Irish-Americans, we can now say that we have augmented our Irish/Spanish/Celtic ancestral genes first with those of the Vikings and second with those of the Normans. If your name is Burke (de Burgh), Clare (de Clare), Lacey (de Lacie), Barry (duBarry), Butler, Ormond, Roche, Powers, or especially Fitz anything (FitzGerald being very prominent, but also FitzRobert[s], FitzThomas, FitzMaurice, etc.), it's highly likely that you have Norman ancestry. *Fitz* was the Norman patronymic for "son of," probably from the combination of the French *fils* and the Latin *filius*. Sometimes the Norman names show up as a series of "Fitz," as in Thomas Fitz Maurice Fitz Gerald. It does not mean "bastard son of," though that is the rumor. That usage was reserved for the king, whose bastard sons were called *Fitz Roi,* or "sons of the king," later anglicized to Fitzroy.

Kilkenny Castle, Ireland, home of the Anglo-Norman Butler and Ormond families.

The Tudor Land Grab: How the Irish Became Beggars in Their Own Land

Whereas the Irish ignored the Plantagenets and absorbed the Normans, the Tudors proved far more difficult to ignore. The first of the Tudors, Henry VII, who took the throne in 1485, was not as problematic as his successor, the fabled Henry VIII. Henry VIII approached Ireland with a triple agenda. First, he feared an alliance between Ireland and Spain that might well put the Spanish fleet too close to British waters. Second, he had recently declared himself head of the Church of England, dissolving his relationship with the pope and the Roman Catholic Church. He saw Ireland as an opportunity to eliminate Catholics and consolidate his control of the Church. Third, he no longer trusted the "old Irish," i.e., the Anglo-Norman Irish who had now become "more Irish than the Irish." He wanted to separate the herd and get trustworthy Tudor loyalists into place in Ireland.

To achieve his goals, Henry VIII began by putting the squeeze on the Anglo-Norman lords. In 1534, he called Garrett Og Fitzgerald, chief of the Fitzgerald clan, to London, where he clapped him into the Tower of London. Rumors reached Ireland that Garrett had been executed. Although they weren't true, Garrett's son (known as Silken Thomas by the Irish for his love of fancy duds) staged a rebellion, the first true revolt against the English of hundreds still to come. The rebellion was squashed. Henry arrested Silken Thomas and five of his uncles and executed them all in 1536.

Meanwhile, in the same year, Henry also made moves to get control of the Church in Ireland. First he required that all bishops and priests swear allegiance to him as head of the Church. Later, he dissolved all the monasteries and convents, making homeless fugitives of the Catholic clergy who did not wish to declare their loyalty to the much-married king.

Then, to keep the population in control, Henry reinforced the Statutes of Kilkenny, expanding them to ban the Catholic Mass for the entire populace and adding that all intermarriage between the English Protestants and Irish Catholics was treason and punishable by death. Under Henry, the statutes, which had largely been ignored, suddenly had teeth. They had the potential to tear whole families apart and keep the native Irish unable to move up or gain wealth and power.

Next, in one of his customary spectacular displays of Tudor hubris,

Henry declared himself Lord of Ireland in 1541. In a country of clans and chiefs, who for thousands of years had elected their own high king (or fought each other for that kingship), this Tudor interloper simply abrogated all rights and traditions. Having thus suddenly taken over the throne of Ireland, Henry launched a two-pronged attack to bring the old Irish and the clan Irish to heel. He sent raiders throughout Ireland to attack the strongholds as well as teams of negotiators to force the Irish to capitulate.

Eventually, they did just that, with forty Anglo-Irish and clan Irish lords and chiefs kneeling to declare their allegiance to Henry VIII. For the privilege of being his liege lords, he bestowed English titles upon them, calling even the great O'Brien and O'Neill chiefs the earl of Thomond and the earl of Tyrone, respectively.

Henry died in 1547, obese, with gout, and having been married six times. Yet by the time he died, Henry had sowed all of the necessary seeds for the hundreds of years of Irish rebellion that were to follow and also set in place the conditions that would eventually allow a terrible famine to nearly destroy the people of Ireland.

Henry VIII: Marriages and Children

- Catherine of Aragon, mother of Mary; Henry annulled the marriage in 1533, then broke with the Catholic Church and declared himself head of the Church of England
- Anne Boleyn, mother of Elizabeth; Henry beheaded her in 1536 after one daughter and two miscarriages
- Jane Seymour, mother of Edward VI; died after giving birth in 1537
- Anne of Cleves, married to Henry only six months; marriage annulled as never consummated in 1540
- Catherine Howard, beheaded in 1542 for an adultery committed prior to her marriage to Henry
- Catherine Parr, married to Henry for four years, until his death in 1547

Henry was succeeded by his son Edward VI, who was only nine years old. Edward's reign was therefore carried out by a Regency Council, who got embroiled in a costly war with Scotland (and here you see just one of the seeds of Scotland's 2014 vote as to whether they would secede from England). After Edward's death at fifteen, his sister Mary (Henry's daughter by Catherine of Aragon, also known as Bloody Mary) came to the throne. Mary tried to forcefully reinstitute Catholicism throughout Britain and Ireland by burning and executing hundreds of Protestants (hence the "Bloody" moniker). She first beheaded her cousin, Queen Lady Jane Grey, in order to take the throne. While you might think that Mary would be good for Ireland (and in fact the Irish hoped that the Catholic persecutions would stop), exactly the opposite was true.

Mary created the first "successful" British plantation in Ireland. To do this, she took land away from Irish clans who had held it for thousands of years (the O'Moores and the O'Connors) and simply plunked British settlers down onto that Irish land. She called the settlements Maryborough and Philipstown, after herself and her husband, and the counties she had stolen Queen's County and King's County. The displaced Irish could either depart, die, or work for the British settlers who had been ensconced on their land.

After Mary's death, her half-sister Elizabeth I (Henry's daughter by Anne Boleyn) took the throne in 1558. Elizabeth was much more religiously tolerant than her Protestant father and Catholic half-sister. She founded Trinity College in Dublin, with a policy to allow Catholic students, at least for its first thirty years, but she continued Bloody Mary's plantation policies, seizing the lands of the earl of Desmond for a plantation.

Can you imagine how much the Irish loathed the Tudors by this point?

Indeed, the abuses had made the country ripe for another rebellion. The next one began in the North under Hugh O'Neill, who had been given the British title of earl of Tyrone. Hugh was very Anglicized, having been brought up and educated in England, but in 1588, in County Donegal, he helped the survivors of a shipwreck of the Spanish Armada. The king of Spain offered help to Hugh, and by 1595 Hugh and his fellow clansmen and neighbors were in open rebellion against Elizabeth I. Their rebellion was to last for nine years!

In 1598, at the Battle of Yellow Ford, near Armagh, Hugh O'Neill and Red Hugh O'Donnell scored a victory against the English, defeating a force commanded by Hugh's own neighbor, Anglo-Norman Henry Bagenal. Later, in 1601, 4,000 Spanish soldiers landed in Kinsale with the express purpose of assisting the Irish in their rebellion against England. The Spanish joined O'Neill and O'Donnell but they were defeated by Elizabeth's commander Lord Mountjoy. The Irish surrendered on March 23, 1603, one day before Elizabeth's death. The results would be devastating for Northern Ireland.

Seeds of the "Troubles": The Plantations of Armagh

James VI, Stuart king of Scotland, became James I, king of England, upon the death of the childless Elizabeth I. After their defeat in 1603, O'Neill and O'Donnell knew full well that their days were numbered, but James (perhaps because he understood the Irish clan system, which was similar to that of Scotland) actually granted both of them pardons for their role in the Nine Years' War and the Battle of Kinsale. However, as payment for their sins, he greatly diminished their lands and the scope of their power. They decided to flee. In 1607, accompanied by ninety-nine followers and family members, they abandoned Northern Ireland and set sail for France, in an event that has become known in Ireland as the Flight of the Earls.

This left Northern Ireland essentially leaderless and wide open to another plantation scheme. James confiscated all of Ulster after the departure of the earls and set up plantations for Scots Protestants, who were to remain segregated from the Irish Catholics. Between 1610 and 1630, James settled more than 40,000 Protestant Lowlanders in Armagh. (Oddly, they were called the Undertakers.) Eventually, more than 100,000 Scots settled in the North of Ireland.

The Irish who remained behind became landless, homeless, clanless, and jobless. But the plantations soon needed more labor and the displaced Irish ended up living on their former land but working for and paying rent to Scots Protestants.

The Scots Protestants were hardworking. They farmed and crafted and built towns and churches. They were also genetically and ancestrally very similar to the Irish people they had displaced, as they were largely descended from the Dal Riata Irish who had either migrated to Scotland in the sixth century or had clan and intermarriage ties with the Western Scots clans throughout that time.

However, the two group's have-and-have-not circumstances at the hands of the British crown never allowed them to discover the fact that they had more similarities than differences.

James' Northern Irish plantation settlement resulted in the "Troubles"—the marches and bombings, wars and rebellions, raids and retaliations between Northern Irish Protestants and native Irish Catholics all the way up until the twentieth century. The displaced Irish would raid and burn the settlements, the crown would retaliate, and on and on it went for hundreds of years.

However, don't ever let anyone convince you that the problem was religious. The terms "Catholic" and "Protestant" may have been the pegs on which the two sides hung their hats, but the reason for the trouble was economic. King James had made beggars and tenants of clans who had lived on the land for thousands of years.

Unfortunately, the crown would later give equally horrific treatment to its own Scots settlers, a subject to which we will return.

10
Oliver Cromwell: The Devil in Ireland

History can tell us the stories of great evil, but it can never explain why or how that evil manages not only to achieve its ends but to gather followers to its purpose. Often, however, there seems to be some sense of purification—religious or ethnic or both—underlying the terrible deeds of fanatics. That was certainly true of Oliver Cromwell, the most hated figure in Irish history.

There are historians and apologists who defend Oliver Cromwell, calling him a masterful military tactician on a par with Julius Caesar or the consummate British politician (although calling anyone a politician might not really be a defense). Some recent historians say that Cromwell has been misrepresented, his atrocities were not so bad, and his followers did things in his name.

However, what Oliver Cromwell did to the Irish is, in the final analysis, simply indefensible.

Oliver Cromwell was a Puritan, a convert to that faith in his thirties. He brought a convert's zeal to his new religion, seeing himself as God's chosen warrior. He particularly hated Catholics.

In 1649, after Cromwell's armies had defeated and executed King Charles I, Cromwell was selected to go to Ireland to put down the Gaelic Wars there and get the Catholic Royalists, who wished for the restoration of the monarchy, under control. He took on the job with relish.

At Drogheda, he immediately put 3,000 Catholic Royalists to death. As for those who remained, he confiscated their lands and then shipped many of them to Barbados as indentured servants or slaves. He massacred women and children and killed all of the Catholic priests he could find.

Next he went to Wexford, where he killed 2,500, including 500 women and children. He burned down all the churches (eventually all over Ireland and Scotland) and executed priests, burning several to death.

What was his defense? He wrote, "I am persuaded that this is a righteous judgment of God upon these barbarous wretches."

Next he began serious enforcement of the Penal Laws, first enforcing many of the old Statutes of Kilkenny and then adding new laws directed almost entirely against Catholics:

- Catholicism was completely outlawed.
- Catholic priests had to leave Ireland or be executed.
- No Catholics could attend school.
- No Catholics could teach school.
- No Catholics could vote.
- No Catholics could hold office.
- No Catholics could marry a Protestant.
- No Catholics could own land; any land they did own was parceled out.

Any Catholic priests who did stay in Ireland had to disguise themselves as gardeners or cattle herders, disappearing into the populace. Many brave priests would hold secret "hedge Masses" or "rock Masses" in the countryside for the Irish who would not relinquish their faith. If these priests were caught, they were killed.

By 1652, no Catholic towns remained in Ireland, and all Catholic armies had surrendered. The country was so devastated that a huge famine befell the Irish, accompanied by wild spread of the bubonic plague. Hundreds of thousands of Irish died.

Meanwhile, Cromwell decided to send all wealthy Catholic landowners "to hell or Connaught." Back in England, he passed the Act of Settlement, designed to strip Catholic landowners of any remaining land and give it to "The Adventurers," who had funded his wars, as well as to Puritans and his soldiers.

May of 1654 was set as the deadline for the resettlement. By this point, more than 600,000 Irish had died in Cromwell's war and more than 60,000 had been sent into slavery in Barbados and Bermuda. The rest were moved to the far western edge of Ireland, to Connacht.

By 1660, Cromwell had redistributed 6 million acres of Irish land. His followers had stripped the country of all its forests, half the population

Near Sligo, in Connaught.

was dead or gone, and only 8 percent of Catholics owned any land. Cromwell shipped the remaining "debris" of orphaned children and Irish undesirables to America. Our American immigration began as a forced expulsion.

The Irish who remained behind were poverty stricken, homeless, or tenants on their own previous lands.

For the next 150 years, even after Cromwell's death and the restoration of the monarchy, the Penal Laws against Catholics were expanded again and again. The Irish people who remained in Ireland did so as tenant farmers, whose primary foodstuff was the potato, the humble tuber that would lead to the third great exodus from Ireland and bring many of our ancestors to America.

11
The Scots-Irish Migration to America

If you are at all mathematical, you probably noticed that the potato caused the *third* great exodus from Ireland. So what was the second? The migration of the Scots-Irish plantation Protestants of the North. When last we encountered them, they had been prosperously settled in Northern Ireland by King James I and, despite attacks by the Irish natives, had established farms and towns throughout Ulster. So why would they leave? The answer is complex, and their settlement in America makes for a fascinating chapter in our own history.

Even before Cromwell, James' son Charles I had increased the taxation on the Ulster Scots, and he tried to force them to become Church of England by putting Anglican clergy in all Presbyterian churches as well as Catholic churches. A small group of Scots-Irish migrated very early in Cromwell's reign, between 1648 and 1649, coming to Maryland and settling around what is now Baltimore.

However, after the death of Cromwell and his son Richard, the restored monarchy would make the situation even worse for the Scots-Irish and, oddly, slightly better for Irish Catholics. King James II, while not giving Catholics back their land, did remove many of the restrictions against their faith. They could also finally be members of the Irish Parliament and Irish Army. Protestants in both England and Northern Ireland were none too thrilled with James. What followed next was called the "Glorious War," between Catholic James II and Protestant Dutch William of Orange.

In Ireland, this war would play out in the Battle of the Boyne, fought in July of 1690 near the Boyne River in Drogheda (where Cromwell had landed years before). Eventually, King William prevailed and took the throne. The victorious Protestants of Ulster Ireland (now

Battle of the Boyne, by Dutch painter Jan Wyck, circa 1693. The original hangs in the National Army Museum in London. (Image used here by licensing arrangement with Art Resource Fine Art Licensing, New York, USA)

known as the Orange Order) celebrated a glorious victory for their newly nicknamed "King Billy" and fully expected that their conditions would improve.

They were wrong.

King Billy's Boys Get Billy-Clubbed

By the 1700s, the Scots-Irish of Ulster had created the finest wool market in the world. They wove soft wools into complex plaids and patterns, much in fashion in many corners of the globe. They were also highly successful in the cattle and linen trades. British merchants found that the competition was depleting their coffers, so they petitioned the king and Parliament. King Billy, i.e., William of Orange, proved remarkably disloyal to his Ulster Scots. Foreshadowing what would happen to the Irish Catholic peasants during the Potato Famine, Parliament passed a series of prohibitive laws:

- The Scots-Irish could not export cattle, pigs, or sheep to England.
- They could not trade with America, either import or export.
- They could not export wool to anywhere in the world except England, who could then resell it on the world market at a higher price.
- When the Scots switched to linen exports, Britain passed a law that they could export only plain linen—nothing patterned, checked, or dyed.

At the same time, Britain went to work on religion. Because they wanted the Church of England to be the official church, they passed laws that excluded Presbyterian ministers from marrying or burying members of their own congregations. Such weddings and funerals were deemed illegal.

Next England began a policy of rack rents, i.e., rents that grew exorbitantly high on the Ulster Scots.

Presbyterian ministers began to take their entire congregations to America. In fact, between 1714 and 1720, fifty-four ships plied the waters between Northern Ireland and America. These were not pleasant voyages. Emigrants faced stormy seas, pirates, and death. Many people on the ships were starving and resorted to cannibalism on the crossing, eating the flesh of the dead.

Many were so poor that they couldn't afford tickets, and so they sold themselves as indentured servants to American landowners for a period of four to seven years..

Nor were the Scots-Irish welcome in America. Residents throughout New England felt that the immigrants were going to eat them out of house and home. Many states concocted schemes for settling the Ulster Scots in buffer zones between the more established colonies and the Indians; such Scots-Irish settlements flourished in Virginia and North Carolina.

The Scots-Irish had interesting relationships with Indians. On the one hand, being used to raids by the displaced Irish Catholics, they were fierce fighters against the Indians, matching cruelty for cruelty. On other hand, there was quite a bit of intermarriage among Scots settlers and Indian tribes in these wilderness regions. One of the best-known stories is that of Mary Jemison, a little Scots-Irish girl whose family was captured and killed by Shawnee. She was later adopted by the Seneca (one of the Haudenosaunee or Iroquois tribes), married into the tribe, had numerous Seneca/Scots children, refused to return to colonial life when she was eventually found, and even negotiated for the Seneca after the Revolutionary War.

Mary was captured living in the wilderness of central Pennsylvania and, indeed, Pennsylvania was the primary residence for the more than a quarter-million Scots-Irish who eventually immigrated to America. For example, a very large contingent of Scots-Irish settled Bucks County, north of Philadelphia. Among those was Presbyterian minister William Tennent, who had emigrated from Northern Ireland. He founded his church (below) on the Neshaminy Creek in what is now Warwick, Bucks County and is buried in the cemetery there. The oldest section of the church dates all the way back to Tennent's founding, which makes it nearly three hundred years old.

Tennent was a fire-and-brimstone Presbyterian preacher, who was responsible for beginning what came to be known as the First Great Awakening, an evangelical movement that eschewed ritual and insisted that its followers abide by a personal code of morality and a personal relationship with Jesus Christ. Not only was Tennent the precursor to

Moland House, in Bucks County, Pennsylvania, housed George Washington and the Marquis de Lafayette, among others, in 1777. The Continental Army of 11,000 was bivouacked on the grounds. Most historians estimate that the army was more than 30 percent Scots-Irish.

Jonathan Edwards, whose *Sinners in the Hands of an Angry God* every American student has read (and likely loathed), but he also founded Log College, the first Presbyterian college for seminarians and the precursor to Princeton University, which would follow in 1746.

Of course, the Ulster Scots were strong participants in the American Revolution, and you can imagine which side they favored, based on the treatment they had received from the British Parliament and king. In fact, history tells us that George Washington and Alexander Hamilton attended services at Tennent's church when they and the Continental Army bivouacked at the nearby Moland House in August of 1777. The church may also have been used as a field hospital.

12

A Diet of Potatoes:
Conditions Ripe for Disaster

Try for a moment to picture your Famine ancestor. We will call her Nora. We will say she is seventeen years old.

Once she was a member of a family—five children, her ma, and her da. Once they had worked for a landlord and planted a lazy bed of potatoes. Once they had been full and happy.

But on the deck of the ship in New York Harbor, she is all alone. Ma died of the typhus, as did her two baby brothers. Their feet turned black and then their legs and at last their faces. Nora has to rock herself hard not to think about it.

Her older sister, Meggie, shipped to Australia when she was sixteen; they needed women there for all the Irish boys who were sent away on the convict ships. Nora had been too young or she would have gone. She and Meggie had clung to each other the day of her departure, Meggie in the new dress and shoes they had provided for her.

"We'll never see each other again," Nora sobbed.

"No," said Meggie, "but we will write and we will keep each other here." She had pointed to her heart.

Thinking of this now, Nora pats the inside of her skirt where she has sewn Meggie's letters. Meggie is now nineteen and married, the letters the only contact Nora has.

For a while, it had been just Nora and Da, both of them growing thinner and thinner. At least they had the cottage. The roads of Ireland were full now of people who had been evicted by their landlords—absentee rich men in England. Their landlord lived in Ireland and had at least refused to evict his tenants.

When they finally got too hungry, Da had insisted that Nora stand on the soup line. "Go to the Quakers now, girl," he instructed her, "because they won't ask you to give up your faith." And she had done as he asked, eating the soup rapidly, her face burning each time with the shame of it.

Then Da died breaking rocks for the Road to Nowhere, trying to earn a few pence to feed them. He simply lay down in that road and died, her big father no more than a skeleton, no more than windy bones, still working even though he had eaten nothing for days.

For two weeks after he died, Nora curled up in the corner of the cottage, her face to the wall, waiting to die. But then the ticket came, the village shopkeeper carrying it to her door.

Her older brother, Will, had gone to America in the second year of the Famine. His plan had been to find work and send for all of them, one by one. And now it was too late for anyone but Nora . . . too late.

Still, she was lucky. Will had booked her passage on an American ship. By now all of Ireland knew what happened to those who took the British ships—the coffin ships. Her voyage had been crowded and smelly, but fewer than ten aboard had died, and though there had been rough weather and fearsome loneliness, the families in the berths around her had watched over her, had worked to keep her safe.

Now she hugs herself and scans the teeming docks.

How would she ever find Will?

She is a country girl from Mayo, and she has never seen so many people in all her days.

From her perch near the railing, she can see ships all up and down the quay. Men in green brocade vests wait for the ship to dock, and she wonders if they too had sent for their sisters. Faces of black and white, young and old—none of them looking like the familiar faces of home—push and shove along the docks. Pigs dart in and out of the melee, and dogs bark at each other's heels. All the dogs of Ireland, and all the pigs, have been eaten long ago.

And then Nora sees him.

Will! Oh, Will! He looks the same, except plumper than when he left Ireland. His face is ruddy and his copper hair gleams in the sunlight. He has lifted his hand to his eyes and is scanning the deck, looking for her.

Nora jumps up and down and waves her arms above her head.

"Will!" she calls. "Tá sé dom! Do deirfiúr Nora. It's me! It's your sister Nora."

But he doesn't seem to see her. And then she realizes why. Not only is she taller and older, but she is thin. The girl he had left had been fourteen years old, plump as a pigeon. This girl is a reed at seventeen, a collection of bones in a threadbare dress and tattered shawl.

Her shawl. Ma's red shawl!

Nora lifts it high above her head and waves it like the bright American flag whipping in the wind on the quay.

She sees Will's face turn in her direction, sees him squint his eyes.

"Nora!" he roars. "Nora, is it you?"

She shoves her way to the gangplank, holding tight to the shawl. Will pushes toward her and lifts her in his arms.

For the first time in three years, Nora allows herself to cry, and Will pats her shoulder awkwardly.

"It's all right, girl," he says. "It's all right now. You're home. Home in America."

Story by Juilene Osborne-McKnight

Famine memorial showing a child at a workhouse door, Enniskillen, County Clare.

Many historians, such as the brilliant Tim Pat Coogan, now call the Potato Famine a genocide—the deliberate elimination of a race and country of inconvenient people. Others say that the Famine was allowed to become as bad as it was because of bureaucratic regulations and failures. Whatever the consensus of history, and whatever the feeling in your own family, if your family came to America from Ireland in the mid-1800s, it is likely that they were what is called Famine Irish, one of the millions of Irish who managed somehow to get out—to Canada or New York or Boston—to escape the obliteration of the Irish at home.

The Potato Famine, as we have always called it here in America, was not a famine of potatoes. It was a famine of compassion, a famine of common sense, a famine of prompt response, and it nearly eliminated the Irish from the face of the earth.

Here in America, we Irish-Americans are 40 million strong, but our ancestors landed here poor, starving, terrified, and unwelcome on both sides of the Atlantic. They worked hard to lose the Irish language, eliminate the brogue, find work, get their children educated, fit in, and become American. They did not talk about the Famine; to do so would have been both shameful and painful.

The fact that they survived at all is a miracle.

Remember that more than a million people had already left Ireland before the Famine started. Ireland's population, however, experienced rapid growth, even after those departures. By1841, the population of Ireland was more than eight million people. In 1871, two decades after the Famine, it was only four and a half million. Those who had not died had left, and when the Famine was over, they kept on leaving by the hundreds of thousands. Certain areas such as Galway, Sligo, and Mayo were extremely hard hit in the Famine years, but all of Ireland was devastated in one way or another.

We have already seen some of the causes of poverty in Ireland:

- The Irish could not be educated, vote, or serve in Parliament. They were illiterate and powerless and most still spoke Irish.
- The Anglo-Irish ascendancy class owned the land that used to belong to the Irish. However, most of the landlords lived in England and relied on agents—think overseers—to deal with the tenant farmers.

- The Irish tenant farmers worked for these landlords and paid them rent, under the watchful eyes of those agents.
- There were deep divides between Catholics and Protestants. By the late 1700s, Protestants owned 95 percent of the land in Ireland despite the fact that the population was 80 percent Catholic. Even well-to-do Catholic landowners were required to tithe to the Protestant Church of Ireland. At the height of the Famine, the Church of Ireland owned 5 million acres of Irish land.

In 1800, this situation became worse with the Act of Union. British prime minister William Pitt managed to convince the Irish that things would function better if Ireland, England, Wales, and Scotland were all united. Even Catholic landowners in Ireland agreed to the proposal, largely because they were promised more representatives in Parliament. However, in practice, things went the opposite way. The independent Parliament in Dublin was dissolved, leaving the Irish fewer representatives and thus no voting-bloc power. Also, no Catholics were allowed to participate until after the Catholic Emancipation Act of 1829, spearheaded by Daniel O'Connell, the Great Liberator.

By 1845, the situation was dangerously unbalanced. The Irish farmers—called cottiers—lived on tiny plots of land in little cottages on the landlords' estates. They raised cattle, pigs, sheep, and numerous grain crops for the landlords. All of that produce and all of the money it earned was exported to England.

Additionally, there was no industrial growth in Ireland. While England had built extensive networks of railroads and was beginning to industrialize, thus creating job diversity, the Irish economy was entirely landlord based and agricultural. Although there were good roads in Ireland and railroads around Dublin, these rural estates could be very remote. The Irish peasants were completely dependent upon the landlord system.

Whole Irish families lived in single-room, dirt-floor cottages with thatched roofs. Animals also often lived in the houses, particularly pigs. These families heated the cottages with turf, bricks of peat cut from the local bogs. The peasants could not read or write, and Catholics, of course, could not attend British-run schools. Children were educated a little in "hedge schools," makeshift meetings of a schoolmaster and local Catholic children outdoors near a hedge.

Additionally, these cottiers had to pay rent to the landlord twice a year. Rent day was called "gale day," and those days occurred in May and November. Because the cottiers were not paid much—if anything—for their farm work, they had to find a way to make additional money to pay the rent. Some sold eggs, others the household pigs. Some of the women sewed or baked. The Irish lived in real fear of rent days because landlords had been known to throw people out of their cottages for failure to pay.

And the Irish peasants had a very limited diet. They ate potatoes—yes, just potatoes.

Believe it or not, potatoes are highly nutritious. They contain vitamins C and B, high quantities of potassium, no cholesterol, and excellent minerals such as magnesium and zinc, and they are filling. You could exist in plump happiness on a diet of potatoes, and our ancestors did.

The Irish ate potatoes—called *praties*—three times a day.

Less than a half-acre of potatoes could feed a family of five for a year, and that is what the Irish planted. The potato originated in the New World but actually came to Ireland from Spain as far back as 1590. By the time of the Famine, the Irish were growing a variety called the "lumper," which was cheap and plentiful. Potatoes could be planted in "lazy beds," long rows that were planted in late spring. Farmers would protect the potatoes with lime and sand and enrich them with manure throughout the summer months. Cottiers were forced to buy and eat expensive oatmeal during those months, but once the potatoes ripened, they were stored in pits and eaten for the next nine months.

The smallest, hardest potatoes were fed to the pigs to fatten them for market, but most historians estimate that a farmer probably ate fourteen pounds of potatoes a *day*, while his wife ate ten pounds.

Life expectancy among the Irish then was approximately forty years.

Irish Potato Options

- Boil them in their skins, then put the pot on the table with salt and mustard. Pull the skins back and dip the potatoes in the condiments.
- Mash them with buttermilk if available.
- Mash them with onions if available.
- Make "colcannon" by mixing mashed praties with cabbage or kale.
- Make potato soup with leeks and milk, or mushrooms if you can find them.
- Make potato bread.
- Fry patties of mashed potatoes.
- Slice the potatoes and fry in lard.

When tragedy struck, this single-food system had no backup plans, no exit strategies, no alternatives. In 1845, potato blight struck the Isle of Wight, jumping from there to England, France, and, by September of that year, Ireland. Regional blights and famines had been common over the years, and in fact this particular blight had appeared off and on in America since 1843, but there, the diet was varied enough to absorb the loss. In Ireland, where the whole peasantry ate but one food, this failure of the potato was complete and devastating.

Although no one grasped the cause of the potato blight then, we now know the potatoes had been attacked by a disease known as *Phytophthora infestans.* At the time, horticulturalists had dozens of theories about how to stop it—removing the potatoes, drying them, covering them with lime, etc. None of those worked because the blight was spread, we now know, by wind and water. Ireland is nothing if not wind and water.

Accounts from the time say that the morning that the disease hit Ireland, people knew it first by the smell—a sickly sweet odor drifting on the wind.

The people brought up the potatoes, which at first looked normal, but when they cut into them, they were an odd shade of purplish-black and the smell was sickening. In the later years of the Famine, the blight was already lingering in the lazy beds, awaiting each planting.

Our ancestors' emigration to America had begun, though they didn't yet know it.

But before they could get out of Ireland, conditions would become so abysmal that it's hard to comprehend the horror—or read about it—even from this distance in time.

13

An Gorta Mor: The Great Hunger

"Here, for the first time, the horrors of the poverty became visible, in the vast number of famished poor, who flocked around the coach to beg alms: amongst them was a woman carrying in her arms the corpse of a fine child, and making the most distressing appeal to the passengers for aid to enable her to purchase a coffin and bury her dear little baby."—James Mahoney, "Sketches in the West of Ireland," published in 1847 as reports from the field with sketches in the *Illustrated London News*

BEGGING AT CLONAKILTY.

The Irish Famine is a polarizing subject, even now nearly two hundred years beyond the event. Scholars accuse and defend, but from our perspective as Irish-Americans, what we want to know is what happened to our ancestors. We want to know how and why they were thrust out of Ireland. We want to know what their lives were like in the old country and what they had to overcome in the new. We want to learn all of the truths that our grandparents and great-grandparents would never discuss, for the awful shame of it. Realistically, of course, much of that knowledge is lost to us.

Often, Irish friends and relatives find Americans to be a bit looney on the subject of our Irishness—our deep ancestral connection to the "ould sod." Our passion for Ireland may be difficult for them to understand, but for American Famine Irish, that connection is rooted in the Great Famine, the forced expulsion of our ancestors from a place they would never see again, and the secrets about the old country that we were never told.

Likely the story was too awful to tell.

Our ancestors did not starve in 1845, the first year of the Famine. They might have been hungrier than usual, but there were some stores and they assumed that the next year would bring a fresh, unblighted crop of potatoes. They had endured mini-famines before.

Sadly, there was actually plenty of food in Ireland; the country was replete with grain crops, cattle, pigs, chickens, and sheep. All of Ireland could have been fed and never gone hungry, except for the fact that every bit of that produce not used by the landlords was exported to England for sale.

To make matters worse, England operated under a series of Corn Laws, which had been put in place as far back as 1815. These were Great Britain's answer to a policy of laissez-faire. They did not want to import cheap grain into Ireland from any foreign market, which would depress local grain prices, so they placed very high tariffs on all imported grain. However, if Parliament was willing to repeal those Corn Laws, England could have imported cheap grain to feed the hungry Irish.

In 1845, prime minister Sir Robert Peel pleaded with Parliament to repeal the Corn Laws. (In England, corn meant any kind of grain crop but not Indian cob corn.) "Good God," Peel exhorted them, "are you going to sit in Cabinet and consider and calculate how much diarrhoea [sic] and bloody flux and dysentery a people can bear before it becomes necessary for you to provide them with food?" He managed to push through the repeal of the Corn Laws in 1846, but Parliament forced him to resign. Before they could do that, however, Peel secretly imported 100,000 pounds of Indian corn from America to feed the Irish. Because corn was not covered by the tariff laws, he was able to get around the law with this plan.

However, there weren't enough mills in Ireland to grind the corn into meal, and the unground corn, which they called "Peel's brimstone," often irritated the already weakened intestinal systems of the Irish. But it was enough to feed half a million people for three months, and they eventually learned to mix it with oatmeal to lessen the intestinal scour.

Peel appointed Charles Trevelyan to handle relief efforts, and this was an error of monumental proportions. Trevelyan disdained the Irish he had been tasked to serve. A bureaucratic micromanager,

Trevelyan visited Ireland only once throughout the Famine years and looked upon the Irish starvation as "suffering from an affliction of God's providence," perhaps because they were Catholic and thus merited God's wrath. He also wrote to Lord Monteagle, Chancellor of the Exchequer, that he saw the Famine as an "effective mechanism for reducing surplus population."

Trevelyan created a public works project designed to put the Irish to work, but he bogged it down in Dublin bureaucracy, and millions had no work and no money. In the early years of the Famine, Ribbonmen—secret societies of farmers—rioted for food and work, but eventually the people were so far into starvation that they lacked the strength to fight. Trevelyan sent 2,000 Royal Dragoons to put down the uprisings and kill the starving men.

Meanwhile, Peel was replaced by Whig prime minister John Russell, who would not import any food or do anything to assist the Irish who were starving in earnest by 1846. They also reinstated laissez-faire by allowing the Irish landlords to export all of their crops, but they required the Irish landlords to create domestic relief efforts. This would eventually result in the Irish becoming homeless.

Eviction

To feed their families and continue to pay their rents, the Irish began to sell off their milk cows. They sold their pigs, spinning wheels, and furniture. They still had a roof over their heads, but their landlords were about to change that situation. Because the landlords were now responsible for tenants, they were also responsible for their rents. It was cheaper by far to evict them and more profitable to replace their little cottages with pasturage for their sheep and cattle.

So that is what they did.

At dawn, the agent arrived with policemen, the Royal Dragoons. Molly heard them first because she was about, feeding the younger ones. Ma was still lying in with the baby. Da had warned them that this day might come, but not now, not with the baby still needing Ma's milk and a roof overhead.

Molly walked into the yard. Already, the police had set up the battering ram that would take down the walls of the cottage—"tumbling," they called it.

"My mother is lying in!" she called aloud. The agent walked toward her, the eviction notice in hand. "The baby is only two weeks old. Please, give us more time."

The agent shook his head. "The woman should have considered that before you failed the rent. Besides, you Catholics breed like rabbits. Now get your possessions out or lose them all."

Molly panicked. She ran from policeman to policeman, begging. Before the last one, a young man little older than herself, she dropped to her knees.

Then Ma appeared in the doorway, the baby wrapped in a shawl.

"Help me, Molly," she said quietly. In the dirt yard before the house, Ma's quiet dignity seemed to affect the officious men more than all Molly's pleadings. They fell silent and regarded her. Molly moved to her side.

"Dress the little ones warmly," Ma said softly. "Bundle them as best you can. Have wee Michael help you to move the spinning wheel to the yard."

"But where will we live?" Molly pleaded.

"Hush now," Ma said, stroking her hair. "Do as I say."

Story by Juilene Osborne-McKnight

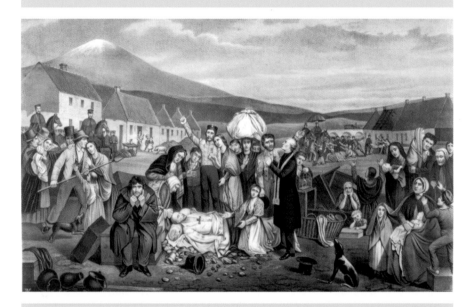

Eviction lithograph by W. H. Powell, 1871. (Library of Congress Digital Collection)

Where the displaced lived was no concern of the landlords or their agents. Often the evictions were preplanned by rack rents—rents that were raised higher and higher until the tenants could no longer afford them.

Many of the evicted Irish were simply displaced to the roads, wandering from place to place and begging. Others went up into the hills and built little shelters called *scalpeens*. Here in America we would call them lean-tos.

By 1847—often called Black 47 because it was one of the worst years of the Famine—the British had enacted a comprehensive Poor Law Extension Act, which contained the Quarter Acre Clause, better known as the "Gregory Clause" after Dublin parliamentarian William Gregory. That clause stated that no government relief whatsoever would be given to a tenant who owned more than a quarter acre of land. This forced families who had no food to give up their homes in order to get something to eat or to go to a workhouse or hospital. By this method, the absentee landlords of Ireland managed to evict more than 250,000 Irish and reclaim their lands for cattle and sheep.

By now, of course, the Irish had eaten all of their domestic animals. Pigs, cattle, sheep, dogs, cats, and rats had been consumed. Men had resorted to stealing sheep from landlord holdings and slaughtering them to feed their families. Hunting or fishing on the landlord's property was strictly forbidden, but men would use slingshots to bring birds down from the air. Whole families foraged for cabbage or turnips, wild mushrooms or leeks, dandelions or ferns.

A truly stomach-wrenching practice called "bleeding" became necessary. Men would slice the neck of a cow and take enough blood to fill a bowl but not kill the cow. The blood was then taken home where it was mixed with mushrooms or cornmeal in order to give the family enough iron to function.

Those who lived closest to the sea fished when they could, but most had sold their currachs—the boats with which they fished—and the dangerous rocky coast prohibited much use of the sea. The starving did boil and eat seaweed, although it often made those unaccustomed to eating it sick, even causing death for some. Some people simply ate the grass; they were found dead in the roadside ditches, green foam around their lips.

By now, disease had begun to spread along with the starvation. Typhus, cholera, and dysentery began taking lives even more quickly than the hunger. Many children were also suffering from scurvy from the lack of vitamin C. Eye infections spread rapidly as well, and many people went blind. Particularly hard hit were children under ten and elders over sixty.

Little children looked like old, old people. They lost all the hair on their heads, and their little arms and legs were like crooked sticks. Their bellies puffed out, a classic sign of starvation. Oddly, downy tufts of hair grew on their faces, a phenomenon we now recognize in those who suffer from anorexia nervosa.

Some of the most heart-wrenching stories of the Famine deal with parents who decided to suffocate their children rather than watch them starve, or who were forced to choose between children, selecting those most likely to survive or feeding older children who could work for the public works and perhaps earn enough to feed the rest.

From the most ancient of days in pre-Christian druidic Ireland, the Irish had always considered the wake and funeral as sacred, guarding the dead for their passage to the next world. Even in the darkest years of the Famine, the poorest families tried to purchase coffins or build makeshift ones from old wood, but eventually too many people died. The hinged coffin came into common use then. The dead person was waked in the coffin, then taken to a cemetery where a trapdoor at the foot of the coffin released the deceased into the grave. The coffin could then be reused over and over again.

Strokestown Park House, near Roscommon, is now a Famine Museum. It is a classic example of eviction and the failure of the landlord-tenant system.

The Mahon family, who were deeded the more than 10,000 acres of land here during the Cromwellian period, evicted more than 3,000 tenants during the Famine, sending many of them away on Famine ships. During the height of the Famine, the owner, Maj. Dennis Mahon, was assassinated, probably by Irish rebels.

In recent years, the massive house was taken over by a car-repair and garage company, but they found hundreds of documents related to the Famine in the tenant office and decided to restore the house instead.

Now American descendants of the Famine Irish can tour the big house, where china dolls still sit at a tea table and riding crops are ready for the hunt. Gorgeous formal gardens include a folly, walking paths, and lily-strewn ponds.

But nearby, in the estate's former stables, a full Famine Museum documents the lack of food, the terrible hunger, and the numbers who were sent away or died. The preserved records show tenants pleading for help and receiving eviction or exile. A visit to this museum is sobering but richly informative.

The formal gardens and lily pond at Strokestown house and the view of the estate from the stable door.

Worhouses: "Indoor Relief"

In 1838, Great Britain instituted an Irish Poor Law that divided Ireland into 130 unions, each of which was supposed to create a workhouse designed to shelter, feed, and employ the poor. The scheme was to be paid for, really, out of the pockets of the poor, as the landlords were asked to use rent money to fund the construction and supply of these structures. Almost every union had one by the start of the Famine, and they estimated that they might well be able to accommodate more than 100,000 poor. By 1846, one year after the start of the Famine, more than 400,000 starving and evicted Irish had taken up residence in the workhouses. By 1847, more than 900,000 needed help.

Unfortunately, help was not always what they received, and the Irish people looked upon the workhouses as the last desperate stop before death. Life in these workhouses was horrific. First, children were separated from their parents, and husbands and wives were separated from each other. Each group lived in a separate ward of the workhouse. The workhouse staff consisted of army men or policemen, and the rules were prison-strict and rigidly enforced.

Before the workhouses were overwhelmed during the Famine, work began at dawn with roll call, after which the inmates ate *stirabout*, a gruely porridge. They worked until noon, were given buttermilk and hard bread, continued to work until seven o'clock, ate potatoes or cornmeal, and went to bed at eight o'clock. Meals were taken in silence. No one was allowed to leave, and infractions of any rules could and did result in whippings.

Men were put to work breaking stones or building roads to absolutely nowhere. Women could sew or knit or do domestic chores. Children were often put to work separating strands of braided hemp rope. Sometimes the inmates would turn the wheel that ground the cornmeal sent from America.

Eventually, the crowded conditions meant rampant diseases, of course. Tuberculosis, whooping cough, and influenza killed many. Dysentery from eating bad food or drinking bad water was rampant, and that meant diarrhea in the workhouses. Cholera was also present, as was an odd virus called "relapsing fever," in which the sufferer would get better, only to suffer a relapse a week later, followed by two or three more relapses. Relapsing fever was survivable, if the sufferer was not already too weak.

Typhus was rampant, and it was a death sentence. It is carried by lice, and the straw bed ticking was infested with them. Lice are also perfectly capable of jumping from person to person. Typhus, called "black fever," would first manifest itself as black toes, and it eventually spread throughout the body, even blackening the face of the victim. Typhus victims stank, and charitable visitors to the workhouses often wrote about the appalling stench. Gangrene would set in at some point, followed by death. The Irish grew so fearful of the black fever that some would escape from the workhouses in the middle of the night to go back to the open road, where they had less chance of catching the disease. Sometimes they abandoned their children in the workhouses. In fact, by the end of the Famine, 40 percent of all children in the Workhouses were either orphaned or abandoned.

Even out in the villages away from the workhouses, families would abandon their cottages if someone inside came down with typhus. They might bring the person food or water, but it was extended into a window on a shovel so as to limit contact.

Priests and clergymen also had very high rates of death from typhus, because they tried to minister to the starving in both the workhouses and the villages.

There were only two options for getting out of this dire situation. The first was death, and hundreds of thousands departed by that route, buried in mass graves right on the Famine grounds. Many of those mass graves are still being discovered now; many show hundreds of children piled on each other, most with evidence of disease and scurvy.

The second exit was emigration. It was much cheaper for a landlord to buy a steerage ticket on a ship departing for Canada or the U.S. and get rid of his burden than to pay to keep his former tenants in the workhouse. By this method, many starving Irish were sent to Grosse Ile or New York. Girls between the ages of fifteen and eighteen might be shipped off to Australia to marry the young men who had deliberately committed crimes to get themselves sent to the penal colonies of Australia, where they would have food.

If you have ever watched Lisa Kudrow's fascinating ancestral series *Who Do You Think You Are?* you might remember the episode in which researchers discovered the workhouse where American actress Rosie O'Donnell's family had been incarcerated until their landlord shipped them out. Viewers could not help but be moved when she entered the stark, abandoned structure and broke down over the shame and horror that her ancestors were forced to endure.

Charity and Soup: "Outdoor Relief"

While the British government was extraordinarily slow to provide relief for the starving Irish people, the British people did step up, as did much of the rest of the world. First to send money was Calcutta, India, a British-occupied territory. Through the combined efforts of both British and Indian people there, 14,000 pounds sterling were sent to Ireland for distribution.

Great Britain proper also formed the British Relief Association, which sent more than 400,000 pounds, and Queen Victoria herself contributed 2,000 pounds sterling and wrote letters exhorting the British people to donate. Most of this money was used to feed children in Ireland's schools.

Pope Pius IX wrote an encyclical asking Catholics around the world to help, and he donated 1,000 Roman crowns to the effort.

Of course, the United States stepped up to the plate, with Irish-American immigrants organizing vast relief efforts. In 1847 alone, the United States sent more than a million dollars of aid. We sent more than 114 ships full of food and clothing. Railroads in the United States would not charge for any materials shipped across the country for Irish Famine relief. Of course, we sent steerage tickets, with many earlier immigrants trying to find their relatives and bring them to America.

Soup kitchens did not come into existence in Ireland until 1847, by which time the starving Irish were dying by the thousands. Great Britain passed the Soup Kitchen Act, which placed outdoor soup kitchens in every one of the 130 Workhouse Union districts, and by June of that year, soup kitchens were feeding more than two million

Irish. In the Western counties of Ireland, in fact, soup was the only source of food by that point.

These soups were not terribly nutritious, and they sometimes brought more problems. There are soup stories in which the cluelessness of the British elite seems almost impossible to believe. For example, the chef at the Reform Club of London, Monsieur Alexis Soyer of France, bragged that he could make a hundred gallons of soup for less than one pound. The recipe contained leeks, barley, flour, water, brown sugar, and beef, but so little of it that it was more of a beef broth; Queen Victoria's own physician decried its nutritional value, and many doctors said that it caused dysentery.

When Soyer's soup kitchen was set up, it was clean and well organized but incredibly degrading. A little bell rang, letting in 100 starving Irish, who ate the soup with a spoon chained to the table, then received a hunk of bread and departed through another door. The spoons were wiped down and the next 100 entered. Worst of all is that on the day the kitchen opened, set up at the Royal Barracks of Dublin, all the wealthy elite of Dublin dressed up and came out to watch the starving people eat, each contributing five shillings toward charity for the privilege of observing the spectacle!

Soyer himself, however, probably does not deserve all the scorn that historians have heaped on him. He fed 5 million people—albeit broth—later wrote a book about the subject, donated all of those profits to charity, and helped to improve battlefield eating conditions for soldiers during the Crimean War. At least he attempted to offer a solution.

Many Protestant groups also set up soup kitchens, but "taking the soup" required a devil's bargain. The Irish Catholics would be given soup only if they would renounce Catholicism and convert to the providing church. Thousands of Catholics took this bargain, and for 100 years after the Famine, their families were labeled as turncoats. In retrospect, this seems excessively sad. As Irish-American parents and grandparents, can we be sure that we wouldn't have converted if it would have allowed us to feed our starving families? However, the motives of the churches who pulled this stunt must be seriously called into question.

The best of the best among the soup-kitchen providers were the Quakers. In a spirit of Christian charity that required nothing in return, they made hundreds of huge pots of soup and created soup kitchens in the Eastern half of Ireland long before the British passed the Soup Kitchen Act. Because there weren't many Quakers in Ireland, they came in from England and Europe. They hired people to work with them and help them. They hired ships and brought in meal, flour, peas from Philadelphia charities, medicine, and clothing. They took seed to hard-hit areas in the West of Ireland and helped the people to plant crops. They gave out money. Our Irish ancestors, and by extension, we Irish-Americans, owe a tremendous debt of gratitude to the Society of Friends.

One of the most moving stories of a nation assisting the Irish during the Famine comes from the Choctaw Indian Nation of Oklahoma. Only fifteen years before our Famine began, an Irish-American president, Andrew Jackson, had forced the Five Civilized Tribes (the Choctaw, Cherokee, Muscogee/Chickasaw, Creek, and Seminole) off their traditional lands of thousands of years, herding them to Oklahoma in the Trail of Tears. Thousands died on the way.

The Choctaw were diminished in numbers and financially strapped, but they managed to raise more than $170—$10,000 today—to send to the Irish for Famine relief.

In 1990, members of the Choctaw Nation marched in the Irish Famine Walk to commemorate the Doolough Tragedy (see below). Two years later, a group from Ireland walked the Trail of Tears Commemoration with the Choctaw. In 1995, Irish president Mary Robinson visited the reservation in Oklahoma and thanked the Choctaw Nation for their sense of "common humanity" with the Irish people.

How a nation so severely depleted and horribly treated managed to think first of our ancestors is a tribute to the spirit of the Choctaw people and worthy of our profound gratitude.

The Doolough Tragedy

Not many people know it, but more people died in 1849, after the Famine was officially over, than in Black 47, long described as the worst year of the Famine.

One of the most haunting tragedies occurred that year near a tiny town on Clew Bay in County Mayo, an area where nearly 100 percent of the population was starving. The people of the town had gathered to meet with two officials who were to decide whether or not the town should continue to receive food relief, but the officials went instead to Delphi Lodge, a British hunting lodge twelve miles away. They sent an order that the people should show up there at 7:00 A.M. if they wanted food. Some historians estimate that more than five hundred villagers made the trip, walking all night in the cold March rain. When they got there, they were turned away.

Many perished on the return trip, dying of hunger at the edge of the road. Most historians think that the dozens who never returned and were not counted among the dead were so thin that they were blown by the wind into the dark and icy waters of Lake Doolough. They were never found.

She is not as tired as some of them who made the long, rainy walk to Doolough earlier today, only to be turned away by the British soldiers, with their disdainful expressions and their bellies full of food. She is hungry, yes, but young and strong. She has not yet resorted to eating the grass.

Night falls along the broken road, and the wind rises.

She continues on among the people, comforting here, holding someone against her there. She takes a small infant from a weary woman and walks along beside her. She looks down into the blanket in her arms. The infant is still and pale. She feels a sudden rush of fear and is surprised as it courses through her, hot and alive. She thought she had forgotten how to fear. She lifts the blanket a little over the baby's face and says nothing to the mother. There will be time enough for that when the sun rises. Here at the crest of this hill under the full moon, with the shining lake below, it would be too much, just too much.

From the front of the line she hears the MacVeagh Mhor, her father.

"Kathleen," he calls back along the bedraggled line. "Are you there, girl? How do they fare?"

"I'm here, Da," she calls back, though the wind is rising, carrying her voice toward the silvered water below. "We are following on."

She does not know how he is walking anymore. Once he was large in more than just his name, a man nearly seven feet tall, muscled and strong. Once he could till a field all day and whirl her mother in circles on the dancing boards. Her heart clenches at the thought of her mother, little brother, and sister, gone now, gone, and her da, so thin, skin stretched over bird bones, his concern all for the people, his own grief held in check as he tries to find them food, like the chieftains of old.

The wind picks up her shawl, tries to snatch it away. She clutches at it with her free arm, yanking it back around her and the dead baby.

Here at the top of the hill, the wind is a living thing, howling, screaming, changing direction on a whim. She leans away from it, then into it. For a moment, she cannot move at all, standing still against its onslaught.

She shelters herself behind a little outcrop of rock, closing her eyes against the howling.

When she opens them, the people are flying—flying—tumbling and soaring, lit by the full moon and heading out over the water, silent.

In the moment before Kathleen understands what is happening, in the moment before the screams begin, she has the fleeting thought that their flight is beautiful, the most beautiful thing that she has ever seen.

"Da?" she calls when the wind subsides. "Da?"

There is no answer.

A wailing begins then among the remaining people, a thin reedy sound like the keening of an uilleann pipe.

Kathleen hands the baby back to its mother. She drops to her knees and crawls to the edge of the cliff.

Far below her, limned in moonlight, she can see the bodies that have been swept over the edge: dozens of them, some crumpled on the shore, some spread-eagled in the water, looking rested and calm, buoyed by the gentle swells of the windswept lake.

Her father is among them.

She rests her head against the cold earth. She wants to fly too, to soar out in the moonlight, to leave this terrible hunger behind.

But she is her father's daughter. And the people are gathering behind her.

Story by Juilene Osborne-McKnight

14

Away, Away to Amerikay

By 1871, when the Famine was "over," the population of Ireland had shrunk to just over four million people, when it had been eight million at the start of the Famine. Yet, historians estimate that about a million people died in Ireland during the Great Hunger. The rest emigrated. Historians estimate that between 1845 and 1855 alone, more than two million people emigrated to the U.S., Canada, Australia, and Liverpool, England, with more than five thousand ships making the voyage back and forth across the Atlantic.

Our ancestors were the "lucky" ones, the ones who found a way to get out. They did that by ship, and the voyages were terrifying. Like the "golden triangle" that moved slaves, rum, and crops from Africa to the Caribbean and America, the new "golden journey" sent Irish emigrants out and timber back.

History does not realize how desperate and hopeless the condition of these Irish emigrants was. One clueless writer of an online monograph comparing Irish Famine sufferers to American slaves said that the Irish's "choice to live or die was their own." Nothing could be further from the truth.

There was no choice. The options were death or death:

- Stay in Ireland and die, either in a workhouse or of starvation, or
- Risk death on the sea journey, but only if they could find some means to obtain a ticket.

Those who lived were both miraculous and anomalous.

In some cases, passage was provided by landlords who wanted to get rid of the Irish. At the very beginning of the Famine, a group of Anglo-Irish landlords had proposed a Celtic colony in Canada, to which they would send 2 million Catholics. This would get the troublesome people out of Ireland, and the proposers of the plan felt that such a colony might preserve all things Celtic. The proposal sounds remarkably like a plan to save certain species in a zoo.

In 1847, when the Famine had reached complete desperation, the landlords who were at a loss as to how to get rid of their tenants returned to the idea of sending them to Canada. The British ships strongly resembled slave ships, except that they were more crowded.

The British government and much of the press were thrilled with this forced evacuation plan. "They are going! They are going!" shouted the rabidly anti-Irish *London Times*. "The Irish are going with a vengeance. Soon a Celt will be as rare in Ireland as a Red Indian on the shores of Manhattan."

There were four ways for our ancestors to depart Ireland:

- An initial journey to Liverpool followed by a longer voyage to America. Liverpool became known as "Little Ireland," because more than a quarter-million Irish who arrived there and received food and shelter were too exhausted to go further. Some never departed. Some worked there for a few years to put together money and then departed for America.
- Booking passage on an American ship, if you had any means at all or if relatives from America could send the ticket. American ships were safer and cleaner and had lower death rates than British ships.
- Getting deliberately arrested and sent to a penal colony in Australia. Conditions on the prison ships were actually much better than on the coffin ships, because there was plenty of food and space. Beginning in 1849, young Irish women were sent to Australia as well, because there were no women there.
- Booking or accepting steerage passage on a coffin ship.

For example, the previously mentioned Maj. Denis Mahon, of Strokestown house, chartered the *Virginius* and *Naomi* to get rid of more than seven hundred of his tenants. These were British ships, still known to this day as coffin ships, in which the poor and starving of Ireland were crammed into steerage below decks in appalling conditions.

The British companies clapped together berth areas that were six feet by six feet. That space needed to hold an entire family and any possessions they had managed to bring with them. There were no bathrooms as such; buckets had to suffice, and in rough weather those overflowed, spilling sewage across the decks. Of course, the holds were filled with cholera, pneumonia, influenza, typhus—brought on board with the very lice that had been carrying it on land, though on board they called it "ship fever."

Passengers were allowed up on deck in the fresh air once a day, and they were permitted to cook over open barrels there. Supposedly, the ships provided rations each day in the form of a pound of bread, rice, flour or oatmeal, or a pound of potatoes plus a quart of water. In reality, those numbers were off, because each coffin ship was overcrowded, sometimes by as much as two to three times the legal limit. The voyage generally took about eight weeks, less depending upon the captain and the weather.

Historians estimate that these coffin ships lost as many as twenty thousand passengers between 1845 and 1855, but that number does not count those who died in quarantine at Grosse Ile in Quebec.

The *Virginius*, for example, left Liverpool with 496 passengers, well over capacity; 158 died on the passage over and were thrown into the Atlantic. (Sharks began to follow these Famine ships on their trips across the Atlantic, anticipating the bodies that would be unceremoniously dumped overboard.) Another 180 were sick on the *Virginius* when they reached Canada and had to be put into quarantine at Grosse Ile. In fact, by 1847, Grosse Ile was overwhelmed, with more than thirty Famine ships waiting in the St. Lawrence River carrying more than 10,000 Famine sick on board.

More than five thousand of the Famine dead are buried on the island, now a Canadian national park where a Celtic cross broods above the scene from a rocky escarpment. The inscription on the cross reads: *"Children of the Gael died in the thousands on this island having fled from the laws of the foreign tyrants and an artificial famine in the years 1847-48. God's loyal blessing upon them. Let this monument be a token to their name and honour from the Gaels of America. God Save Ireland."*

The Miraculous *Jeanie Johnston*

Jeanie Johnston was the only ship to make it all the way through the Famine without ever losing a passenger. How did she accomplish this? Generally, Capt. James Attridge did not overload the ship, although he did once carry 254 passengers (the ship's capacity was 40). However, Dr. Richard Blennerhassett, of Edinburgh, swabbed the ship down with lime to diminish disease, required the passengers to get fresh air, and aired the bedding. The ship brought 2,500 people to America with not a single death and even the healthy birth of a baby boy on board.

The ship was reconstructed in 2002 and toured ports in New York and Philadelphia as well as Canada.

In addition to ship fever and starvation, there were other dangers for our ancestors on their voyage to America. Ships foundered in storms and sank, some within sight of the English and Irish coastlines. Others caught on fire and burned or were struck by lightning. Of course, there were massive and terrifying storms at sea that poured icy salt water down the hatches. Several Famine ships hit icebergs. The worst of those stories was the tale of the *Hannah*.

In 1849, the *Hannah* hit an iceberg. Her twenty-three-year-old captain, Curry Shaw, fled in a lifeboat, but while 49 died, the ship *Nicaragua* picked up 129 survivors the next day, all of whom had been standing on the iceberg in their nightshirts. The BBC ran a story on the sinking in 2011 (*The Ice Emigrants*) that detailed the horror of the event and the awful cowardice of the crew.

In all, more than 650,000 of our ancestors made their way to North America. Most of those who were released from quarantine in Quebec continued on to America, while those Irish who arrived directly came into the Port of New York. By 1850, more than 25 percent of all New Yorkers were Irish.

Although you might think that the generous Americans who had assisted in the Famine would be happy to welcome the starving Irish to their shores, the number of immigrants was just too overwhelming for American cities. Our ancestors experienced staggering slums, child mortality rates of 50 percent, and the terrible prejudice of job postings declaring "No Irish or Dogs" and "No Irish Need Apply," but they were alive. And they were the toughest of the Irish—the ones who had survived. Their odyssey will be the subject of our next chapters.

Perhaps one of the saddest aspects of their migration is that those of our ancestors who did leave living relatives back in Ireland knew that they would never see them again. Families would stage "American wakes" on the night before departure. A fiddler would play tunes, and those who could would dance their final *ceilidh* in Ireland and look for the last time at the stars over Ireland. Sometimes, families would engage professional keeners and they would stage the *na caoineadh*, the wailing, in which they would weep and lament over what Ireland was losing—its brave young men and women, its next generation.

In fact, in those years of the Famine and its aftermath, Ireland nearly lost everything and everyone. And we Irish-Americans, even this many generations later, lost something too: the history of our families, the long story of our people, the sense of being woven into the fabric of our past. For our ancestors did not just leave Ireland; they were torn from it like a piece of fabric torn into halves—torn hungry, dirty, and desperate from their families, their land, and their history. The half they left behind became a shame, a secret, a story never to be told. The half that landed on this shore would have to fight for more than a generation to be whole again—to be, at last, American.

For Further Reading: An Annotated Bibliography

Nonfiction

Bartoletti, Susan Campbell. *Black Potatoes: The Story of the Great Irish Famine, 1845-1850.* Boston: Houghton-Mifflin, 2001.
Bartoletti offers a children's book that does not mince words or details about the Great Famine. It is well organized and illustrated with good, specific examples and stories from the Famine period.

Coogan, Tim Pat. *The Famine Plot: England's Role in Ireland's Greatest Tragedy.* New York: Palgrave Macmillan, 2013.
In this indictment, Tim Pat Coogan accuses the British government of deliberate genocide during the An Gorta Mor, particularly under the Whig party and Charles Trevelyan.

Cusack, George, and Sarah Goss, eds. *Hungry Words: Images of Famine in the Irish Canon.* Dublin: Irish Academic Press, 2006.
This is a series of essays by a variety of Irish and American scholars who are looking at images of the Great Famine in Irish fiction, poetry, and plays.

Dolley, Michael. *Anglo-Norman Ireland, c1100-1318* Dublin: Gill and MacMillan, 1972.
Dolley has penned as dense and turgid a book as you will ever read—he presumes that you will know all of the O'Briens, O'Tooles, and MacMurroughs who fought each other for land and eventually lost it to the Normans—but the whole story of the "invited invasion" is here if you can wade your way through the clan politics.

Edwards, R. Dudley. *Ireland in the Age of the Tudors.* New York: Barnes & Noble Books, 1977.

The chapters are divided by subheads that do not follow a chronology, so you must be well informed about Tudor Ireland before reading.

Ellis, Peter Berresford. *Hell or Connaught!: The Cromwellian Colonisation of Ireland 1652-1660.* New York: St. Martin's Press, 1975.

Although this book jumps around somewhat chronologically, it is a repellant and fascinating study of religious fanaticism combined with unlimited power. By the end of the book, the death of Cromwell and the deposition of his equally horrific son come as a profound relief, even for readers who already know the horrors that he heaped upon our ancestors.

Ford, Henry Jones. *The Scotch-Irish in America.* New York: Arno Press, 1969. First published 1915 by Princeton University Press.

A very thorough study of the Scots emigration and its causes is followed by extensive information on Presbyterian universities and churches founded by the Ulster Scots-Irish.

Foster, Roy, ed. *The Oxford Illustrated History of Ireland.* Oxford: Oxford University Press, 1989.

This overview of Irish history is well illustrated with good explanatory maps.

Gallagher, Thomas. *Paddy's Lament, Ireland 1846-1847: Prelude to Hatred.* New York: Harcourt Brace, 1982.

Gallagher focuses on the seeds of Irish hatred for the British based upon the worst two years of the Irish Famine.

Hayden, Tom. *Irish Hunger.* New York: Roberts Rinehart, 1998.

This is a unique and thought-provoking collection of essays and poems by both American and Irish writers on the subject of the Great Famine.

Kee, Robert. *Ireland: A History.* Boston: Little, Brown, 1992.

Kee focuses on the "Troubles" in Northern Ireland by unpacking, era by era, all of the repressions and outside decisions that made them inevitable.

Keegan, Gerald. *Famine Diary: Journey to a New World.* Edited by James Mangan. Dublin: Wolfhound Press, 1991.

This is a diary of the journey of a schoolmaster and his wife on a coffin ship to America. The diary makes really compelling reading, but there is a caveat. Evidently James Mangan, a Christian Brother, added, deleted, and changed material, fictionalizing much of it. There was an original diary in 1895 called *Summer of Sorrow,* but some scholars say that was later subjected to heavy edits. Read this one as if it were fiction.

Laxton, Edward. *The Famine Ships: The Irish Exodus to America.* New York: Henry Holt, 1996.

Laxton's text is a seminal and eminently readable book that looks at the terrible conditions on the voyages to America and at the equally awful conditions for the arriving immigrants. Particular focus here is on Irish-owned ships manned by Irish crews. It includes fascinating details, such as passenger manifests and price lists, and a center section of color plates.

Litton, Helen. *The Irish Famine: An Illustrated History.* Minneapolis: Irish Books and Media, 1994.

This excellent, clear, and well-organized study of the Famine is illustrated with sketches and supplemented with letters and newspaper accounts from the time.

Maxwell, Constantia. *The Stranger in Ireland: From the Reign of Elizabeth to the Great Famine.* London: Alden Cape, 1954.

Maxwell's unique book is a compendium of essays and letters by travelers of every nationality who passed through Ireland, from the period of the Tudor repressions all the way through the Famine. It is fascinating to see history through their eyes. The letters and essays are full of prejudgments and prejudices as well as sympathy and the lack thereof.

McCarthy, Karen F. *The Other Irish: The Scots-Irish Rascals Who Made America.* New York: Sterling, 2011.

This is a delightfully fascinating study of the first Irish migration of the Ulster Scots Presbyterians in the early 1700s. This book is so well written that it reads like a novel and makes the characters and journeys of the Ulster Scots comprehensible and compelling.

Moody, T.W., and F. X. Martin, eds. *The Course of Irish History.* New York: Roberts Rinehart, 1995.
  Each scholarly essay in this collection is dedicated to a certain period in Irish history, summarizing it and analyzing its causes and effects.

Moran, Patrick Francis. *Historical Sketch of the Persecutions Suffered by the Catholics of Ireland Under the Rule of Cromwell and the Puritans.* Dublin: M. H. Gill and Son, 1884.
  Written by the archbishop of Sydney, this is a thorough, though linguistically turgid, recitation of Cromwell's persecution of the Irish Catholics.

Neill, Kenneth. *An Illustrated History of the Irish People.* Dublin: Gill and MacMillan, 1979.
  If you can find a copy of this book anywhere, it honestly is as lavishly illustrated as promised and you will dip into it repeatedly.

Ó Gráda, Cormac. *The Great Irish Famine.* New York: Cambridge University Press, 1995.
  This very unusual little book looks at Malthusian and economic theories surrounding the Great Famine.

Ranelagh, John. *Ireland: An Illustrated History.* New York: Oxford University Press, 1981.
  This coffee-table book features excellent photographs and maps.

Woodham-Smith, Cecil. *The Great Hunger: Ireland 1845-1849.* London: Penguin Books, 1992.
  Cecil Woodham-Smith was an Oxford-educated female historian and resident of England, but Irish by virtue of being a Fitzgerald of Anglo-Norman ancestry. She was perhaps the first to indict the British for their handling of the Irish Famine, and her book is the basis for works by many other writers.

Fiction

Giff, Patricia Reilly.
  Her young-adult fiction trilogy—*Nory Ryan's Song, Maggie's Door,*

and *Water Street*—follows Nory Ryan through famine, emigration, marriage, and life as a New York immigrant.

Kelly, Mary Pat. *Galway Bay*. New York: Grand Central, 2009.
    Kelly's extraordinary novel tells the story of the Kelly family, who have to flee Ireland to Chicago during the Great Famine. This epic brings the factual material to life with memorable characters and events.

Llwelyn, Morgan. *Grania*. New York: Forge, 2007.
    This novel is based on the true story of Grania O'Malley, an Irish woman pirate of the Tudor period who actually met Queen Elizabeth I.

——. *Strongbow*. New York: Tor, 1997.
    The stories of Richard de Clare Pembroke and Aoife, daughter of Dermot MacMurrough, alternate here.

O'Connor, Joseph. *Star of the Sea*. New York: Mariner Books, 2004.
    O'Connor's novel takes place on a ship crossing to America during 1847, known as "Black '47" during the Great Famine. A mystery, love story, and vengeance story intertwine for a compelling read.

O'Flaherty, Liam. *Famine*. Dublin: Wolfhound, 2002.
    This is a heart-wrenching novel about the complete demise of a large Irish-Catholic family in Galway, Ireland during the Famine. O'Flaherty shows the reader the atrocities of the estate overseers, the efforts and failures of the Church, the British indifference, and the horrific results.

Video

The Manions of America. DVD. Directed by Charles Dubin. First released in 1981. Entertainment One, 2012.
    Although there are soap-opera elements to this television miniseries, which stars Pierce Brosnan and Kate Mulgrew, it personalizes the story of the Irish working class and the English landlords whose lives were forever altered by the landlord/tenant system and the Great Famine.

When Ireland Starved. DVD. Films for the Humanities, 2003.

This informative and detailed set of four documentaries—*Causes of Poverty, Managing the Famine, The Irish Holocaust,* and *Exodus*—explains the causes and exacerbations of the Famine as well as the emigration to America, Canada, and Australia.

Irish Roots and Rising Irish
The Irish Become American

Part IV: Irish Roots and Rising Irish: The Irish Become American

15
Pre-Famine Irish Catholic Immigrants

The wave of Catholic immigration to America actually began a number of years before the Famine, during the 1820s. Most historians estimate that more than 150,000 Irish Catholic peasants came to America in the two decades prior to the failure of the potato crop. It would be interesting, from this distance, to question those early immigrant ancestors about why they came then and how. Did they foresee a time when Ireland would starve? Or were they aware that the landlord/tenant system had such a low ceiling that they would never be able to rise out of poverty as long as they stayed there? It must have taken all the resources they could muster to buy a ticket and get even one family member out.

Of course, when someone did make it to America and find work, they began a domino effect of bringing other relatives over—saving money to send back for a sister or brother, until, one at a time, the whole family made their way across the water.

Although the number of these early arrivals did not overwhelm the ability of America to absorb them, they were nonetheless unwelcome. They were poor, uneducated, and illiterate. They were willing to work hard, but most spoke Irish as their primary language, and worst of all, they were Catholic. It is nearly impossible to overestimate the prejudice that adhered to being Catholic, as we will see in this chapter.

One early incident that illustrates not only this prejudice but also the complete misunderstanding of the religion was the burning of an Ursuline convent and school in Charlestown, Massachusetts in 1834. Somehow, Protestants in the region became convinced that the nuns were holding women in the convent against their will. A mob gathered and burned the convent to the ground, forcing the nuns to escape with their students.

Such prejudices against nuns were also fueled by lurid literature about convents, such as *The Awful Disclosures of Maria Monk,* published in 1836, a supposed autobiography of a trapped Montreal nun who claimed that priests had constructed secret tunnels in order to carry on illicit affairs with residents of the convent. She also wrote of physical abuse and a burial tunnel for unwanted babies. Later investigations proved that she had never lived in the convent and, in fact, had resided for years in an asylum, after which she went on to a career in prostitution. However, such books were extremely popular, spawning an entire genre and an avid readership of scandalized American and Canadian Protestants.

Of course, Protestant immigrants from Ireland, Britain, and Germany had brought their anti-Catholic prejudice with them, and America's early Puritans were also anti-Papists. To be fair, we must acknowledge that Protestants were not that far removed from the Reformation, a movement that occurred largely in response to corruptions in the Catholic Church. They were predisposed to see Catholicism as fundamentally corrupt. Early American Protestants feared that the pope had ruling designs on America, a belief that persisted all the way until the presidential campaign of John F. Kennedy!

Remember the Irish who had migrated from Scotland in the 1700s? They had risen in society and were successful and well regarded by this point. So they were the first to distinguish themselves from the newcomer Catholic rabble, electing to call themselves Scotch-Irish and eventually altering that to Scots-Irish or even Scottish.

Such attitudes made it difficult for the early Irish Catholic immigrants to find work. They were willing to take on the very worst of jobs—hard, manual labor in coalmines, digging the canal system throughout America's East Coast, and building the railroads. These were the only jobs they could get because newspaper postings for household staff or shopwork often concluded with the sentence "No Irish Need Apply."

By the early 1800s, thousands of Irish were busily employed digging the canal system designed to connect the Great Lakes with Eastern rivers. Irish diggers who built the Illinois-Michigan canal settled in Chicago, creating a huge Irish population in that city, many of whose descendants live there still. All told, Irish workers dug more than four hundred miles of canals across the Northeast.

Interestingly, Irish and black workers were segregated on the canals because it was believed that the Irish would be a bad influence upon the Africans. British actress Fanny Kemble was married to an American named Pierce Butler, who owned numerous plantations and kept slaves. Fanny, who was a prodigious writer, kept extensive diaries and letters. In one of her entries in 1838 or 1839, she noted that any contact between the Irish and the slaves would cause "tumults, and risings, and broken heads, and bloody bones, and all the natural results of Irish intercommunion with their fellow creatures." But

The Delaware Canal was a 60-mile stretch of the 1,200-mile Pennsylvania Canal system. It was begun in 1829 and built almost entirely by Irish immigrant labor. Now it is the Delaware Canal State Park and can be hiked or biked. In its functional days, mules, led by mule boys on the path, pulled barges from section to section, with the boatman blowing on his conch shell to warn the lockkeeper of his arrival. Lockkeepers often lived in little houses beside the canal.

The Usual Irish Way of Doing Things, by cartoonist Thomas Nast. Originally appeared in *Harper's Weekly*, 1871. (Image used here by licensing arrangement with Art Resource Fine Art Licensing, New York, USA)

many of our early Irish ancestors were themselves prejudiced against Africans, both slave and free, perhaps perceiving, and not liking, the fact that the larger population saw both groups as similarly inferior. More practically, they were afraid that the Africans would take the jobs they themselves were scrabbling to hold.

By the late 1800s the Irish were widely portrayed in the newspapers and magazines of the time as apelike drunkards, especially by cartoonist Thomas Nast. In fact, it was widely believed that the Irish were a genetically inferior nonwhite race (and the vast array of prejudices in that statement alone is frightening), a view that persisted into the early 1900s.

Of course, this situation was about to get much worse, as America would be inundated with a million starving, ill, Irish-speaking, illiterate, and nearly hopeless Irish Catholic Famine refugees.

16

The Incoming Tide

Raggedy Irish immigrants descend the ship's gangway to America in this detail from the Famine Memorial by Glenna Goodacre, installed in 2003 on Penn's Landing in Philadelphia.

More than three-quarters of all the Irish who came into Canada on the coffin ships eventually made their way into the United States.

We could properly say that Grosse Ile was their first port of entry to America.

Here in the States, Famine immigrants arrived in droves in numerous port cities. The National Archives show ships' manifests for arrivals of more than 500,000 Famine Irish to the Port of New York alone!

Ports of Entry: Irish Famine Immigrants

- New York > 750,000
  - Prior to 1855, Hudson and East River docks
  - 1855 to 1890, Castle Garden, developed to keep good records and protect immigrants from dockside "runners"
  - 1890 to 1892, Barge Office
  - 1892 to 1924, Ellis Island
- Boston > 250,000
- Philadelphia
  - The Lazaretto, a quarantine island in the Delaware River
- New Orleans
- Baltimore

Remember that the Irish were leaving a farming life, a rural life of wind and stars, even if it was repressive and hungry. These were not urban dwellers; they had no idea of how to go about living in a city. We tend to think that our ancestors arrived and took up farming in the Midwest, but the truth is that more than three-quarters of all Irish immigrants ended up in the cities, where they overburdened resources and became very unwelcome squatters.

Naturally, in the early years of the Famine, none of the ports was set up to receive that number of immigrants, and the conditions they came into made them easy marks. "Runners" wearing Irish vests and speaking with a familiar brogue would warmly greet the bewildered, sick, and starving immigrants. The well-fed, cheery ambassadors, once of dear old Ireland, would direct them to tenement slums, where they would have a roof over their heads and food to eat—at least according to the patter of the runners.

The reality was far less charming. In the slums of the Five Points area in New York, more than a thousand people could often be crammed into a five- or six-story building. Multiple Irish immigrants lived in a single apartment. There were no jobs and the conditions were filthy, with open sewage running in the streets and no garbage collection. Irish children who lived—and infant mortality was extremely high—ran wild throughout New York like packs of dogs, young women turned to prostitution, and the separation from the old land and old ways caused severe depression and alcoholism. Of course, the slums were also rife with tuberculosis, typhus, cholera, pneumonia, and every other close-quarters disease of the poor.

Often the slums were so crowded that the new immigrants were forced to build shelters out of debris. These came to be known as "shantytowns." If you grew up Irish and Catholic, you know well that even up to the post-World War II generation, our own parents differentiated the Irish as "shanty Irish" or "lace curtain Irish," phrases that came into existence in the slums of cities such as Boston, New York, and Philadelphia.

So many Irish were arrested during this early immigrant period that the New York police nicknamed their arrest wagons "paddy wagons." "Paddy," in fact, became the pejorative label for all Irish men and "Bridget" or "Biddy" for all Irish women.

There was terrible violence in these Irish slums. Five Points had first been occupied by emancipated slaves, and there was no love lost between them and the Irish. The new Irish immigrants knew that the established classes considered the black workers better behaved and more trustworthy.

Worse still was nativist violence against both groups, but in particular the Irish. Nativists called themselves Native Americans. They considered themselves the original Americans, though they bore no relationship ancestrally or historically to actual indigenous American Indians. These nativists hated the dirty, illiterate, slum-dwelling Irish and directed violence at them repeatedly. The Irish formed gangs—calling themselves such names as "The Forty Thieves," "Dead Rabbits," and "Kerryonians." These criminal enterprises also battled Protestant nativist gangs such as the "Bowery Boys." Martin Scorsese captures this dark and violent period in Five Points in his film *Gangs of New York*.

This nativist/Irish violence was not confined to New York either. Kensington was Philadelphia's Irishtown. Here, in May of 1844, there were three days of gun battles between Protestant nativists and Irish

Catholics. The violence got so bad that the Protestants burned down St. Michael's Church and St. Augustine near the Ben Franklin Bridge.

So the question becomes: how did our ancestors rise out of ignorance and poverty?

The simple answer was hard work, but in fact, ten major factors allowed our immigrant ancestors to fight their way out of poverty and despair. They were:

- Building and construction jobs
- Transportation jobs
- Steel mills, coalmines, and goldmines
- Labor unions
- The American Civil War
- Tammany Hall politics
- The law
- Domestic service for women
- The textile trades for women
- The Catholic Church

We will unpack each of these factors and look at how they served as ladders out for our ancestors.

17
Our Ancestors "Get to Work"

Bridges and Tunnels, Bricks and High Iron:
Irish Workers in New York

In the city of New York, our ancestors took any and every backbreaking labor job that was available to them. They became hod-carriers and bricklayers. Bricks are laid out grid-style in a hod (a trough on a pole), and the hod-carrier hoists it over his shoulders and moves the bricks from the brick site to the building being erected. Big Irish laborers were known for their ability to carry heavy hods. Once their skill and tirelessness at carrying hods became known, our ancestors became bricklayers, helping to construct New York's great buildings.

They also erected the Brooklyn Bridge between 1869 and 1883, side by side with German and Italian immigrants. An interesting side note is that Boss Tweed of Tammany Hall offered a lot of bribes (often called "good graft" historically) to get the bridge project off the ground. We'll return to Tammany Hall and its politics later.

The Brooklyn Bridge was once called the "Eighth Wonder of the World." It joined Brooklyn to Manhattan across the East River, but it had to be built by going under the water of the river in "caissons." These were iron "rooms," shaped like bell

Icarus High on the Empire State photograph, by Lewis Hine. (Image used here by licensing arrangement with Art Resource Fine Art Licensing, New York, USA)

jars, that were dropped below the water and pumped full of air so that the men could work under water. Many developed nitrogen narcosis in this environment, the agonizing condition that scuba divers call the bends. Others died by falling off the towers or being struck by falling stone.

The high-iron workers who built the Empire State Building were also Irish. There they labored side by side with Mohawk Indians (Haudenosaunee Iroquois) in conditions that would be considered unacceptable today unless you were daredevil tightrope walker Nik Wallenda!

In contrast to working in the sky, our ancestors (and indeed many modern New Yorkers) also toiled under the ground as "sandhogs" when New York built subway systems and underground tunnels.

Out of the City and Onto the Rails

In 18 hundred and 41,
work on the railroad had just begun;
work on the railroad had just begun;
working on the railroad.

Patsy orey orey ay,
Patsy orey orey ay,
Patsy orey orey ay,
Workin' on the railroad . . .

1842, '43, '44

In 18 hundred and 45
found myself just barely alive,
found myself just barely alive,
from working on the railroad.

In 18 hundred and 46,
I sadly dropped four dynamite sticks;
I sadly dropped four dynamite sticks
while working on the railroad.

In 18 hundred and 47,
found myself at the gates of heaven,
found myself at the gates of heaven,
after working on the railroad.

Irish and Chinese workers built the railroads of America in a great race to meet in the middle.

The Central Pacific Railroad came east from Sacramento; at one point their workforce was more than three-quarters Chinese. The Chinese were indefatigable, unafraid to use dynamite, never drunk and disorderly, and, according to the History Channel, immune to dysentery because they brewed green tea.

The Union Pacific Railroad came west, employing primarily Irish Civil War veterans (we will talk about the Civil War later). The Irish laborers were at high risk for attacks from Native American war parties, who wanted to stop the railroad that was impinging upon traditional hunting grounds and decimating herds of buffalo. Because these Irish workers were Civil War veterans, they were also more likely to agitate for better wages and conditions, although the railroads often put such strikes down with brutal tactics.

On April 28 of 1869, a group of unnamed Chinese laborers and a

Railroad Building lithograph, by A. R. Waud. (Library of Congress Digital Collection)

group of Irish railroad workers with names such as Kennedy, Egan, and Daley laid more than ten miles of track in a single day and brought the Eastern and Western U.S. together, cutting the cross-country trip from more than six months to six days.

The Transcontinental Railroad was not the only railroad built by the Irish, however, who built local spurs across the U.S. and all over the East Coast. Many died and were buried in unmarked graves, while others rose to staggering wealth and prominence.

Diamond Jim Brady. (Library of Congress Digital Collection) Brady is a fascinating Irish railroad success story. The son of poor Famine immigrant parents, he began his working life as a messenger boy for New York's Central Railroad. Brady must have had the innate ability of our ancestors to observe and imitate, because by his early twenties he had become the chief assistant to the railroad's general manager. He later became vice-president of Standard Steel and went on to amass a fortune as a salesman of railroad supplies. By the time of his death in 1917, he owned a gorgeous wardrobe and the first car in New York. By modern estimates, his jewels alone would be valued at more than fifty million dollars. He was a legendary glutton known for eating the finest lobster, beef, and chocolate, a fact that is bittersweet when one considers that his childhood and that of his immigrant ancestors must have been so hungry. However, he didn't smoke, didn't drink, and never married, though he kept company with the actress Lillian Russell.

The Tragedy of Duffy's Cut

Sister John Marie leaned over the young man and drizzled water into his lips. Her white wimple cast a winged shadow over his face, but John Marie knew that was not the only shadow over the young man. She leaned close.

"What is your name, lad, and I will write home to your parents."

"Ruddy," he whispered. "John. My people are in Donegal."

John Marie patted his hand gently and stood.

The tiny shanty was full of young men in the deep throes of the cholera. All of them were Irish, all of them Catholic, abandoned here to die.

John Marie bit hard on the insides of her cheeks to stifle a sob. Two of her sisters had accompanied her here today and she watched them move among the young men, whisper a prayer, and provide water, their winged wimples lifting and dipping like the wings of the Holy Spirit. The cholera had come to Philadelphia months before, but when it reached these young men, no medical care had been forthcoming and no sympathy, surely, for these boys were Irish, immigrant, and Catholic—the poorest of the poor—railroad navvies all.

Only her order, the Sisters of Charity of Mother Seton, would come among these poor sick children, and John Marie knew that even their gentlest care would be useless.

She reached down along her side and fingered the thick black rosary beads that hung from her belt.

"Mother of the suffering Lord," she whispered, "take these children home."

Story by Juilene Osborne-McKnight

The story of Duffy's Cut is at the opposite end of the railroad spectrum from Diamond Jim Brady. In 1832, long before the Famine, a railroad boss named Philip Duffy, of the Philadelphia and Columbia Railroad, hired fifty-seven young Northern Irish immigrants to lay railroad line about thirty miles west of Philadelphia on a section of railroad that was to be part of the main line from Philly to Pittsburgh. For a very long time, the story of how these men died was kept in a locked railroad vault. But in the late 1990s, Lutheran minister Dr. Frank Watson and his twin brother, Dr. William Watson, of Immaculata University found the papers and were eventually able to authorize an archeological dig.

What they found was a mass grave of dead Irish boys, but even more shocking was the discovery that some of the young men had been murdered, either by blunt-force trauma or by bullets. One theory is that local nativist anti-Catholic vigilantes killed them. Some of the bones have been identified and belong to men bearing names such as McIlheaney, Skelton, and Devine; those have been given Christian burial and a marker in a cemetery in Bala Cynwyd, Pennsylvania. DNA evidence has linked John Ruddy to his descendants in Donegal and he has been sent home for reburial.

In another sad coda to the story, our fictional Sister John Marie could not have imagined that her own convent would be burned to the ground in anti-Catholic rioting in Philadelphia in 1844.

Duffy's Cut: For Further Study

• Immaculata University has a Duffy's Cut Museum in their gorgeous Gabriele Library.
• WNET, PBS New York, has done a riveting documentary on the tragedy called *Death on the Railroad.* You can stream it from Gabriele Library's Web site.
• The Drs. Watson have written a fascinating book, replete with details of both the search and the mystery surrounding the deaths of the navvies, entitled *The Ghosts of Duffy's Cut: The Irish Who Died Building America's Most Dangerous Stretch of Railroad.*
• Legendary Irish folksinger Christy Moore has written a lovely folksong entitled "Duffy's Cut." You can stream it on YouTube.
• The Irish punk-rock band the Dropkick Murphys have written a heavy tribute called "The Hardest Mile," alluding to the fifty-ninth mile, where the Irish boys are buried. You can also stream this song on YouTube.

Under the Ground

By the early 1900s, there were more than 600,000 coalminers in the United States, working in two types of coalmines—anthracite and bituminous—with most of the anthracite mines being owned by the railroads.

Not all of these miners were Irish. In fact, there was a distinct pecking order in the mines, with British and Welsh miners being held in higher regard than the Irish, but with Italian and Eastern European miners ranking below the Irish, once they began to immigrate. There was no love lost among any of these groups, with each group living in its own "ghetto," attending its own church, and strictly forbidding fraternization among the groups, a condition that persisted in Pennsylvania's coalmining towns until well after World War II.

Of course, the conditions in these mines were terrible. Some American mines required that miners be eighteen to go beneath the ground, employing the younger boys as "breaker boys," children

Breaker Boys in Pennsylvania Coal Mine photograph, by Lewis Hine. (Library of Congress Digital Collection)

who worked separating coal from slate and rocks and breaking up large chunks. However, other mines used small children under the ground as collier's boys, cart boys, and trap boys—little children who sat alone in the dark, opening and shutting trapdoors.

Pennsylvania's coal towns, as an example, were all mountainous and remote, so there was very little in the way of education or opportunity. We all remember the line from the folksong "I owe my soul to the company store," and in fact, miners lived in company-built housing, bought all of their essentials at the company story on "scrip," and ended up with a tab. In these "patch towns," the company also ran the church, infirmary, post office, and school, effectively trapping their workforce within their system.

If you are interested in seeing a true patch town firsthand, in Pennsylvania, you can visit the restored Eckley Miner's Village. Near Scranton, you can also experience the conditions deep below the earth by going into the Lackawanna Coal Mine.

Of course, the conditions in the mines were extraordinarily dangerous. Mines collapsed and exploded, and older miners often died from black lung.

In 1875, Pennsylvania miners organized the Long Strike to lobby for safer conditions and better wages, but when the governor called in the military, Irish miners resorted to the guerilla tactics that had been used against the English landlords back in Ireland, giving rise to the Molly Maguires.

Because the Irish were distrusted and disliked by the English and Welsh, as well as by the mine bosses, a number of far-reaching changes began to occur, typified by the story of the Molly Maguires. One of these changes was the eventual development of labor organizations such as the Workingman's Benevolent Association and the United Mine Workers, founded in 1897 as an early and very powerful American union and still in existence today.

The Story of the Molly Maguires

Historians are deeply divided on the Molly Maguires. Some say that they never existed, while others say that they were a subdivision of the Ancient Order of Hibernians, who came to the United States in 1836 and become a national network for Irish Catholic immigrant workers. A few say that they hearken back to the Ribbonmen of Famine Ireland, the disenfranchised landholders who harassed and murdered English landlords.

In any case, Irish miners in the mountainous coal country of Pennsylvania began to harass mine owners, mine police forces, and mine bosses in protest against wage reductions and terrible conditions in the mines and the mine-owned towns. Some historians say that they committed at least fifty murders; others claim three times that many.

The Philadelphia and Reading Railroad owned the Philadelphia and Reading Coal and Iron Company. Franklin Gowan was president of both companies and owned more than half of the coalmines in Eastern Pennsylvania. He decided to retaliate against the Mollies by hiring the Pinkerton Detective Agency and having them place a mole in the Mollies' secret operations. That mole was a detective named James MacParland, who infiltrated the organization as James MacKenna and collected information against the Mollies. However, a group of vigilantes began to kill off the Mollies before their cases came to trial, even killing the wife of one of the Mollies. That death proved too much for MacParland, who resigned, though Pinkerton eventually persuaded him to remain on the job.

More than twenty Mollies were arrested and tried, although they were arrested by the mine police, and Franklin Gowan set himself up as the special prosecutor on the case. Obviously, they stood very little chance of a fair trial. Over the next two years, twenty Mollies were found guilty and hanged.

The Hand of the Mollies

In cell seventeen of the Carbon County Jail in Jim Thorpe, Pennsylvania, the history of the Molly Maguires shadows the wall. There, Alexander Campbell, tavern owner and member of the Mollies, protested his innocence of the murder of John Jones and Morgan Powell throughout the long months of his trial.

On the day that he was to be hanged, he pressed his hand into the dirt and slapped it against his cell wall, declaring that his handprint would remain on the wall forever, to remind everyone that an innocent man had been hanged.

Some legends say that at one point a sheriff tore the wall down and replaced it, only to have the hand reappear. As late as the 1960s, another sheriff painted over the wall, or so he says, only to again have the hand reappear.

Tourists visit the site now, where the shadowy handprint of Alexander Campbell, Molly Maguire, reminds us, at the very least, of our ancestors' difficult assimilation into the American melting pot.

Silver and Gold

When a huge chunk of gold was found in a riverbed at Sutter's Mill, California in 1848, the Irish began to flood California. Many Irish had already moved to the San Francisco area long before, but the gold rush swelled that number to more than 4,000 by 1852 and more than 30,000 by 1880. In fact, by 1880, the Irish comprised 37 percent of the population of San Francisco.

Of course, not all of those adventurers became rich on gold, but

Gold Miners in El Dorado California circa 1850. (Library of Congress Digital Collection)

the Irish were political animals, and in the young West, they became organizers, planners, and doers. They eventually elected the first Irish-born mayor of San Francisco, Frank McCoppin, as well as an Irish governor of California in H. H. Haight.

One Irishman who did strike it rich during the gold rush was James Phelan of County Laois, who owned a successful dry-goods business in Cincinnati. However, Phelan struck it rich on dry goods! He bought mining and "camping" equipment, sent it to California on three ships (one of which sank en route), and set up shop. He made a fortune almost immediately and then parlayed that money into successful banking, insurance, and construction ventures. Eventually, his son James Phelan became governor of California and served in the U.S. Senate.

Four Irishmen actually did strike it rich on silver. Called the "Bonanza Group," this foursome discovered the richest vein of the fabled Comstock Lode, discovered in 1859 in Nevada. Together James MacKay, James Fair, James Flood, and William O'Brien produced more than $100 million worth of silver. Eventually they formed the Virginia Mining Company and went on to increase their fortune in silver stocks and banking.

The Irish in Steel

Big Steel—the primary driver of American manufacturing—lasted from before the Civil War until the 1970s, with companies dying a sudden death or fading out as they failed to modernize and manufacturing moved overseas.

In its heyday, American steel was the production leader of the world, producing more than 60 million tons of steel annually and supporting hundreds of thousands of steel-related industries as well as immigrant workers and their families.

Our Irish ancestors were a big part of that steel story, although steelworkers included Italians, Poles, Hungarians, Czechs, Russians, and eventually Hispanics and African-Americans.

Many of you probably grew up as descendants of Irish steelworkers in such cities as Pittsburgh, where Andrew Carnegie owned the largest set of steel operations in the world; Bethlehem, Pennsylvania, where Charles Schwab (yes, that Charles Schwab) made Bethlehem Steel the second-largest operation in the world; and Youngstown, Ohio, where

The ruins of the Bethlehem Steel Stacks in Pennsylvania, once populated by Irish and European immigrant steelworkers.

the combined forces of U.S. Steel, Republic Steel, and Youngstown Sheet and Tube made that region a powerhouse of steel and the third-largest producer in the U.S. Chicago also had a huge steel presence, with a large number of Irish workers.

For those of you who grew up in any of these steel towns, you remember well the sparking red of the night skies as the blast furnaces turned out their products, followed by the sooty gray of the daytime skies, when the debris of steel production polluted the air. You remember fathers who worked twelve-hour shifts, sometimes in the middle of the night, in boiling-hot and dangerous conditions surrounded by molten steel and fire. You know that several generations of many families went "into the mill," with sons following in their father's footsteps. You probably also remember that the entire population was Catholic but your schools and parishes were often segregated, with the Irish, Italians, and Eastern Europeans all moving in different church and social circles. Such was the world of the Big Steel Town.

When Big Steel died, whole cities or areas of cities died with it.

Some cities, such as Pittsburgh and Bethlehem, wisely diversified, while others never succeeded in that attempt. The failure of Big Steel has meant that many Irish were forced in re-emigration, leaving towns where their families had lived for more than a century in order to find work in other areas of the United States.

Youngstown, Ohio: A Case Study in the Death of Big Steel

- Founded in 1797, the area first drew Irish immigrants who mined coal and dug the Erie Canal.
- By the mid-1800s, the town boasted three iron and coal companies and employed hundreds of Irish immigrants.
- By the twentieth century, the town lay claim to three major steel companies, U.S. Steel, Republic Steel, and Youngstown Sheet and Tube. The area experienced rapid economic and population growth, with workers of Irish, Italian, Eastern European, and African descent in the mills. During the heyday of steel in the early1970s, the population of Youngstown and Mahoning County exceeded 300,000.
- On Black Monday, September 19, 1977, Youngstown Sheet and Tube closed, followed over the next ten years by all other steel operations. Ten thousand jobs disappeared in a matter of days.
- Thousands more jobs were lost, hundreds of corollary companies closed, and the area became known as the Rust Belt.
- The population of the county is now below 234,000, a decline of nearly a quarter of the population.
- Youngstown proper declined from approximately 140,000 residents in 1970 to 65,000 currently.

Biddy in the Big House: Irish Women in Domestic Service

By several years after the Famine, the pattern of emigration from Ireland had shifted; more women than men began to immigrate to the United States. Most of them found work as domestic servants. In fact, in her fascinating book *The Irish Bridget: Irish Immigrant Women in Domestic Service in America,* author Margaret Lynch Brennan tells us that by 1900, more than 50 percent of all domestics in the U.S. were Irish.

The rich and famous—such as the fabulously wealthy Vanderbilts, writers Emily Dickinson and Mark Twain, and politician Theodore Roosevelt—frequently employed Irish female domestics.

Try to imagine what this must have been like for an Irish immigrant girl from post-Famine Ireland. She misses her family terribly, writing letters home weekly. But she lives in a heated house, perhaps one wired for electricity. Maybe she has her own room. She wears a crisp clean uniform and can bathe and wash her hair. She has enough food to eat.

Moreover, she sees sumptuous décor and gorgeous dresses and hats. She hears the conversations of industrialists and statesmen and raises the children of heiresses. She serves table at fabulous dinners with five or six pieces of silverware per setting and fine cut crystal.

In the way of all the Irish, she watches, learns, and imitates.

The Biltmore Mansion in Asheville, North Carolina. The Vanderbilts were just one of the well-off American families who employed Irish housemaids, cooks, and nannies.

Some employers, such as Edith Vanderbilt, provided schools for their domestic servants, who learned to read and write in addition to being trained in fine manners.

Irish domestics were so ubiquitous in these wealthy homes that, as a group, they were simply nicknamed "Bridget" or "Biddy." In fact, for many of the well-to-do, it became a mark of social class to employ Irish servants as well as to complain to others in your circle about their feisty stubbornness or lack of knowledge and social graces.

Margaret Lynch Brennan says that Irish domestic servants were largely responsible for Irish assimilation into the mainstream culture, because once they saw what passed for good manners and high society, they did their best to imitate, both before and after they married.

Photos of Irish domestics from the period show them dressed for Mass and a Sunday out in fine outfits and huge, feathered hats, in imitation of fashionable high society. For most "Biddies," Sunday was their only day off, if their employer allowed one, and Mass was the social center and meeting place. The result was that Irish domestic women contributed money to their parishes.

They also managed to save money and send it back to Ireland. Many scholars estimate that from the time of the Famine to the turn of the century, Irish domestic girls sent more than a quarter-million dollars home to Ireland, either to help the folks there or bring a brother or sister to America.

Mill Girls: Irish Working Girls in Cloth Trades

As the Industrial Revolution got under way in America, textile mills, such as the ones in Lowell, Massachusetts, began to employ women as early as 1820. Although many of these women were American and Protestant, as the industry grew, the mills also began to hire female Irish Famine immigrants and French-Canadian immigrants. These workers came to be known as Mill Girls or Factory Girls.

While conditions in these mills were difficult, with the women working twelve- to fourteen-hour days, the mills became one of the interesting passages into American society for three reasons:

1. The mill owners offered classes and lectures, and many Mill Girls took advantage of them, bettering their reading skills and knowledge.
2. Mill Girls lived together in boardinghouses, often six to a room.

These had strict curfews and codes of behavior and were often presided over by "house mothers." The girls received three meals a day, and they ate together in a common room. Although the girls worked hard and were exhausted, the boardinghouses must have offered an atmosphere similar to a women's dorm at a university, with the girls making new friends from a variety of backgrounds, trading books and life experiences, as well as helping each other through life crises.

3. Mill Girls formed the first women's labor union. Called the Lowell Female Labor Reform Association, they petitioned for ten-hour workdays in 1845. Although this was declined, they managed to secure a thirty-minute reduction by 1847 and a reduction to an eleven-hour day by 1853.

Thus, our Irish women ancestors were able to be independent in America, improve their education, and learn that agitation for change, unlike in the Ireland they had left, actually did (though slowly) produce results in America. Too, like the domestics, Irish Mill Girls could save money to send home for their brothers and sisters.

18

Politics as a Ladder: Tammany Hall to the White House

To understand how and why Irish-Americans became involved in politics, we have to go back to the nativist anti-Irish sentiment that we mentioned earlier.

You will remember that nativists often fought battles with Irish gangs in New York, Boston, and Philadelphia, a condition that was well portrayed in Martin Scorsese's *Gangs of New York*. Such riots even occurred in St. Louis, Missouri.

In addition to considering the Irish dirty, drunken, brawling, and illiterate, nativists harbored frightened suspicions about their Catholic religion, believing that the pope wanted to take over America and turn it into a papal state. In Philadelphia, for example, the riots of 1844 got started because members of the Native American Party, which had become, by this time, an organized political party, became convinced that Catholics were trying to remove the Bible from the public schools.

At that time, public-school days began with a reading from the King James version of the Bible. A Philadelphia bishop had asked the schools for permission for Catholic students to read from a Catholic version, and the rumor mill exaggerated the story into complete removal of the Bible from schools (sad to think that this goal was eventually achieved anyway, but that is a modern tragedy rather than an Irish one). In the Kensington section of Philadelphia, then an Irish ghetto, a group of nativists held a rally that was attacked by the local Irish. Three days later, the nativists returned with greater numbers, and fighting broke out. The three-day riot resulted in several nativists being shot and the convent of the Sisters of Charity (home of our fictional Sister John Marie in our Duffy's Cut section), St. Michael's

231

Church and rectory, and St. Augustine's Church being burned to the ground. Three months later, riots broke out again in Philadelphia, centered around St. Philip Neri Church.

Interestingly, all three parishes still exist, having been rebuilt, and a couple of them tell the story of the nativist riots on their Web sites. After these riots, Catholic churches in Philadelphia took to building (or rebuilding) with windows so high off the ground that neither bricks nor flaming missiles could be thrown through them.

The Native American Party reorganized itself as the American Party in 1849. They quickly became known as the "Know-Nothings," because all of their members, who were rabidly anti-Catholic and anti-Irish, claimed to know nothing about those prejudiced social positions. Among other things, the Know-Nothings wanted a halt to immigration, a two-decade waiting period for citizenship, and a restriction on any foreign-born person holding public office.

The party actually achieved remarkable success, putting forty-three members into Congress and running Millard Fillmore for president. Eventually they fell apart over the issue of slavery, with anti-slavery Know-Nothings joining the Republican Party and pro-slavery Know-Nothings aligning with the Democratic Party. Though this wasn't precisely true, these developments led the Irish to believe that the Know-Nothings became the Republicans—white, Protestant nativists not welcoming of the Irish—thus moving the bulk of the Irish toward the Democratic Party.

> You might be interested to learn that the Ku Klux Klan was not always an anti-black organization. While the Klan emerged after the Civil War and focused on the racial divide, its second growth took place during the 1920s and spread to the Midwest. The Klan then was white Protestant and its entire program was anti-Irish and anti-Catholic, especially in industrial and steel towns with high numbers of immigrants moving into various jobs.
>
> This was also the period in which the Klan began to burn crosses, which they saw as a symbol of Catholicism, something they had not done against blacks after the Civil War.

Meanwhile, the Irish were making inroads into the corrupt Tammany Hall machine that ran New York politics, and while this might not seem like a good thing, it actually helped our ancestors move up in several ways.

Tammany Hall began in the 1700s, long before the Catholic famine Irish immigrated. Incorporated in 1789, this political organization named itself after Tamanend, a Lenape Indian chief, and called their meeting place a "wigwam" and its leaders "sachems." (Such weird appropriations help to explain why many Native Americans are upset by team names such as the Washington Redskins.) Early Tammany Hall used saloons as its social and meeting centers but also strongly supported the temperance movement.

Tammany Hall had the backing of Aaron Burr and quickly became a powerful political machine, not averse to graft as a method of getting its candidate elected. It began to take in Irish Protestant immigrant members. In 1828 it backed Andrew Jackson for president, and he thanked it by giving it control over a number of federal jobs. By 1855,

Interior of Tammany Hall, decorated for the 1868 convention. Lithograph by W. C. Rogers. (Library of Congress Digital Collection). Tammany Hall was a real "hall" on Seventeenth Street at Union Square in New York.

34 percent of New York's voters were Irish, both Catholic and Protestant.

Beginning in the 1850s under the notoriously corrupt Boss Tweed, Tammany became *the* political machine of New York, controlling elections, judges, and political appointments all the way into the 1930s.

For our New York Irish ancestors, however, Tammany Hall often served as a combination of the Saint Vincent de Paul Society, the Salvation Army, and a job fair. Tammany watched out for its constituents, advancing them money when they had none and making sure that they received coal or food or clothing for their children. It set up committees to assist the Irish with getting citizenship. In return, the Irish simply had to become Democrats and vote for the candidates that Tammany told them to vote for. You might remember being told in your childhood that some member of your family was a "lever-pulling Democrat." Tammany is where such nicknames were born.

When Boss Tweed was finally arrested in 1872, Tammany Hall was taken over by Honest John Kelly, who wasn't really all *that* honest but who was Irish, Catholic, and related to the bishop of New York. For the purposes of the Irish immigrants in New York, Kelly's ascension was huge. It meant that Irish Catholics could move into that all-important area of our ancestors' rise to power—the law. By 1880, the Irish had elected the first Irish Catholic mayor of New York in William Grace.

Moreover, using the Tammany system of jobs and political placements, Irish Catholics became policemen and firemen by the hundreds. New York formed a police force in 1845, but Catholic Irish immigrants were not welcome because Tammany Hall was still Protestant, as was the ruling class of New York. However, by 1863, when the draft riots occurred during the Civil War (we will discuss these later), more than half of the New York Police Department was Irish; by the turn of the century this figure was over 70 percent! Naturally, these officers eventually worked their way into every aspect of the law: law school, the FBI, politics, and eventually the White House in the person of John F. Kennedy.

Those of you who remember Kennedy's election remember that his campaign was still surrounded by a significant amount of anti-Catholic, anti-Irish, antipapal sentiment, but his victory—no matter what you thought of his politics—meant that at last the Irish could triumph over those stereotypes and become full participants in American life.

Many estimates say that at least two hundred claddagh rings have been found at Ground Zero of the destroyed World Trade Center, an indication of the still-Irish character of New York's residents.

Others estimate that more than 20 percent of the police and firefighters who died at Ground Zero were also Irish, perhaps working in the same profession as their fathers and grandfathers before them.

Irish America Magazine did a fascinating article in 2011 that focused on the Irish-American and new Irish immigrant composition of the construction force at the new World Trade Center, at right.

Claddagh rings (see claddagh symbol at right) have existed in Ireland since the 1700s and are worn by many Irish-Americans.

The heart represents love, the hands friendship, and the crown loyalty.

Worn on the right hand, the ring indicates that the wearer is single if the point of the heart angles down the fingers, or in a relationship if the point angles toward the heart.

Worn on the left hand, the claddagh indicates that the wearer is engaged or married.

19
Fighting for Amerikay:
The Irish in the Civil War

More than 150,000 Irish immigrants fought for the Union side during the Civil War; more than 50,000 fought for the Confederates. Some sailed to America quite deliberately to sign up to fight, while others were recruited into service when they landed or, later, into one of the legendary Irish brigades. Whatever the reason, they became renowned as the "Fighting Irish," and their service to their new country was a major pathway toward full acceptance as Americans.

But it was a pathway that exacted a heavy toll.

Many of our ancestors were recruited into the war effort as they walked down the gangway of the boat. They were offered a uniform, boots, a weapon, a financial bounty, and good food. Men who had survived the Irish famine and somehow found the means to get themselves to America may not have had anything in the way of starter income or job prospects. Likely, military service looked promising.

Michael Corcoran lithograph, by Currier and Ives. (Library of Congress Digital Collection)

However, many more Irish recruits were brought in by Irish military leaders, including Col. Michael Corcoran and Capt. Thomas Francis Meagher. Both had been fiery Fenians back in Ireland.

Though his father was an officer in the British Army, Corcoran was a Ribbonman (we discussed these secret Irish rebels earlier) who emigrated to New York in 1849 and joined the Sixty-Ninth New York Militia, becoming a colonel by 1859. In 1860, he nearly tanked his military career simply by refusing to march his regiment in a parade to honor the visiting Prince of Wales. He was slated for court martial when the Civil War broke out. Because Corcoran had a loyal Irish following and could recruit more Irish to the war effort, the court martial was lifted. He marched the Sixty-Ninth to Washington, where they participated in the Battle of Bull Run in 1861. He was also a member of the Fenian Brotherhood secret society here in America.

Thomas Francis Meagher lithograph, by Currier and Ives. (Library of Congress Digital Collection)

Thomas Francis Meagher is one of those archetypal Irish whose story would make a stunning novel (and indeed there may be one out there). Born in Waterford to a wealthy family (his father was mayor of the town), Meagher studied in England and France, helped to design the Irish flag, and led the Young Irelanders Rebellion in 1848. For that latter offense, he was arrested and condemned to execution by hanging, but because of public outrage, the British commuted the sentence to exile in Tasmania in Australia (then called Van Dieman's Land).

Meagher married there and eventually escaped (first politely informing the authorities that he intended to do so). He ended up in San Francisco, then made his way to New York, where he became a famous speaker and journalist. He eventually joined the army of the Union, recruiting for New York's Fighting 69th. He rose to the rank of brigadier general and petitioned for permission to start the Irish Brigade, which would grow to include the 63rd New York, 69th New York, 88th New York, 28th Massachusetts, and 116th Pennsylvania.

The Brigade fought under its own flag (green with a gold harp) and the soldiers wore shamrocks in their caps. They had their own chaplain, Fr. William Corby. They fought in more than forty Civil War campaigns, including Bull Run, Fredericksburg, Chancellorsville, Gettysburg, Spotsylvania, and Appomattox Court House.

General Pickett wrote to his fiancée about Gettysburg, "Your soldier's heart almost stood still as he watched those sons of Erin fearlessly rush to their deaths. The brilliant assault on Marye's Heights of their Irish brigade was beyond description. We forgot they were fighting us and cheer after cheer at their fearlessness went up all along our lines!"

But, oh, the cost: over the course of the Civil War, more than four thousand men of the Irish Brigade died for the United States of America. Moreover, they were not remotely the only Irish unit to fight in the war. On the Union side, there were heavily Irish corps in New York, Massachusetts, Ohio, Illinois, and Indiana. On the Confederate side, Alabama, Georgia, Louisiana, and Virginia fielded predominantly Irish regiments. The tremendous bravery of these soldiers raised the respect of the American public for the Irish and helped to ease the prejudice against our ancestors.

Meagher resigned his commission in 1863, frustrated because he wanted to return to New York to recruit more Irishmen for the brigade. Eventually, he ended up as governor of Montana and died by drowning in the Missouri River in 1867. Historians remain deeply divided about Meagher, some calling him a poor leader or drunkard while a strong contingent defends him. Some conspiracy theorists think his death was suspicious.

Michael Corcoran, by then a general, died in 1863 in a fall from his horse and was heavily mourned by the Irish in both the North and South.

Of course, as we know, not all was emerald flags and battlefield glory in the War Between the States. In fact, one of the tragic consequences of the number of Irish who fought in the Civil War was orphaned children—thousands of them—who lost their fathers on the battlefield and their mothers to childbirth or early death.

While some orders of nuns and priests founded orphanages, most of these children were sent to the Midwest to be adopted into non-Irish farming families. This process had been going on since before the Civil War, but the numbers ballooned to more than a quarter of a million after the war. While some orphans found loving families, many were used as cheap farm labor.

A Civil War Christmas Eve Tale
Story by Juilene Osborne-McKnight

Though this famous story may be apocryphal, it is considered a true Irish tale.

On one Christmas Eve during the bloody war between North and South, the Confederate and Union armies were camped on opposite sides of a river and enjoying a Christmas truce. Soldiers had come down to the water's edge to wash out their clothing and camp gear.

Through the darkness and over the water, a Union soldier heard the sad notes of a song he recognized from home.

"My young love said to me,
'My mother won't mind. . . . '"

Mustering his voice, he sang back through the darkness:

"'And me father won't slight you
For your lack of kind. . . . '"

For a moment, there was silence over the water, and then a voice called, "Where are your people from, soldier?"

"Tipperary," the Union soldier called. "And yours?"

"From Cork, mine." The Confederate soldier paused. "God bless you on Christmas, brother."

"And you and all your people," the Union soldier called back.

"I'll wish you well in the battle," responded the Confederate soldier.

"And you," called the Union soldier. "When the war is over perhaps we'll share a pint!"

"Sure, that would be best for both of us, friend," the Confederate soldier replied, and he went away whistling, a sweet sound from home.

Behind him, a long Christmas Eve silence stretched across the deep divide of the water.

Certainly, one of the most ignominious events of the Civil War occurred in New York City in 1863, the same year as Michael Corcoran's death.

The New York City Draft Riots of 1863

In 1863 the United States passed a draft law for the first time in its history. This law exacerbated the already high tensions among blacks, German immigrants, and Irish immigrants in New York City. By this time, more than a quarter of New York City was composed of German immigrants and more than a quarter of Irish immigrants. These two groups feared the black residents of New York, but that fear was based less in race than in economy.

In particular, the Irish and the blacks were competing for the same jobs. There had already been a riot and attack on blacks by the longshoremen in 1863, and when the Emancipation Proclamation went into effect in January, the Irish immigrants were panicked that blacks would take their jobs. Then the draft was announced and blacks were exempted from it, largely because they were not considered fit to be citizens, despite the Emancipation Proclamation.

Their exemption enraged the Irish, who discovered that same week that a rich man could pay $300 to avoid the draft lottery, forcing another, poorer man into service. Thus the Irish, trapped between the rich whites and poor disenfranchised blacks, were drafted.

The first draft lottery took place on July 11, and on July 13 chaos erupted. Irish mobs beat John Kennedy, superintendent of police, to a bloody pulp. They killed Col. Henry O'Brien, who had turned a howitzer on the crowd, slaying a woman and her child. They attacked the homes of rich Republicans, whom they saw as responsible for the draft laws. They burned and looted Brooks Brothers. They attacked the *New York Times*, where the journalists manned Gatling guns!

Then they turned on the black population. They burned the Colored Orphan Asylum to the ground. They beat, hanged, and mutilated eleven black men and, over a period of months following the riots, drove the black population out of Manhattan into Harlem and Queens.

In all, the riots lasted for five days, killed more than 125 people, created racial tensions between Irish and black residents of New York City that have never gone away, and did the Irish a real disservice by making them appear just as bad, depraved, and incorrigible as the elite and the press had portrayed them to be. Some historians now say that the rioters may not have been as completely Irish in composition as the papers of the day indicated, that type of propaganda having been ongoing in the press for more than a decade.

Oddly, one area of the city that didn't really participate in the riots was the Five Points slum, which we have mentioned before. It was a racially mixed neighborhood of German, black, Italian, and Irish residents, with the Irish making up more than half of its population.

Draft riots also took place in Staten Island, Queens, the Bronx, and Boston but all to a lesser degree.

More than 150 years later, scholars still struggle to understand the draft riots. Blacks and Irish were at the bottom of the social strata, were both considered substandard human beings, were competing for the same jobs and were being propagandized to hate and fear each other. No less a dignitary than Frederick Douglass formed a fast friendship with Daniel O'Connell. (You will remember him from chapter 12 as the Great Liberator, who secured the vote for Catholics.) When Douglass toured Ireland, and found it highly favorable to the Emancipation, commented on the divide between the Irish and the blacks in America, writing: "Perhaps no class of our fellow citizens has carried this prejudice against color to a point more extreme and dangerous than have our Catholic Irish fellow citizens, and no people on the face of the earth have been more relentlessly persecuted and oppressed on account of race and religion than have this same Irish people. The Irish who, at home, readily sympathize with the oppressed everywhere, are instantly taught when they step upon our soil to hate and despise the Negro. They are taught that he eats the bread that belongs to them."

Whatever history eventually decides about the 1863 draft riots, it must have been a terrifying and sorrowful five days in Civil War New York.

20

The Parish and the Catholic Church: Helping the Irish to Rise

The gorgeous Celtic-cross altar in the Cathedral Basilica of Philadelphia. The altar is dedicated to the memory of Archbishop Patrick Ryan of Tipperary, who served Philadelphia from 1884 until 1911. A statue of St. Patrick stands at the left, and Archbishop Ryan certainly followed in his footsteps, founding more than 150 churches and eighty schools, including Catholic churches for Eastern Europeans and African-Americans. Ryan's tenure typifies the growth of the Catholic Church in the nineteenth century.

You were born into the parish, were baptized in the parish, made your first Communion and Confirmation in the parish, were married in the parish, and were buried in the parish cemetery.

Everyone you knew was Catholic, and you greeted new acquaintances with a single question: *What parish are you from?*

Often, you baptized your children in the same parish. They were taught in the Catholic schools by orders of nuns: the Sisters of Charity of Mother Seton, the Ursulines, the Dominicans, the Humility of Mary, the Holy Names, and the Notre Dames.

Your children called their nuns by nicknames. Chuck, Aggie, and

Tessie were short forms of Mary Charles, Mary Agnes, and Mary Theresa. Sometimes the names were designations of great affection for loving nuns who kept up discipline and interest in classrooms of more than fifty students. Sometimes they were derogatory terms of terror associated with knuckle-slapping orders. Your children went to mandatory Mass one weekday morning each week. The girls wore hats or mantillas or, in later years, doilies or Kleenex pinned to their hair. All of the students wore uniforms—shirts and ties for the boys, plaid skirts or jumpers for the girls. Discipline was first, last, and always important.

You did not attend Protestant services or Protestant weddings, but you might well have some Protestant friends and you worried about them, particularly about their path to heaven.

If you grew up Catholic in New York, Philadelphia, Chicago, or Pittsburgh, this description might sound exactly like your life in the 1940s, 1950s, and 1960s. Our ancestors in the nineteenth century would also have recognized many elements of that description.

Many modern American Catholics look back on this period in our history with great nostalgia. It was an insular world, certainly, but one in which there was a sense of belonging, safety, and moral certainty.

The whole system was begun by the Catholic Church in large measure to save their Irish immigrants—not only from the bigotry and hatred that was directed toward them in America but also to save them from themselves. The Church worked to bring them out of the degradations of alcoholism, prostitution, and crime but also out of poverty, ignorance, and despair. In large measure, the Catholic Church remade their constituents into respectable citizens.

Many of us who are modern Irish Catholics are quite frustrated with our Church. Some have left; others remain doggedly in membership for the sake of faith and perhaps hope, all the while agitating for change, embarrassed by priest scandals and frustrated with the exclusion espoused by the Church. But it is important for us to remember that if we are Irish-American, Italian-American, Hispanic-American, or Eastern Euopean Catholics, the Catholic Church provided our ancestors with spiritual, financial, educational, and protective services unparalleled by any other American institution.

The Catholic Church in America was mostly Irish in nature, not Roman. This was because most of the priests—75 percent by some scholarly estimates—were Irish born or, later, of Irish descent.

Fighting Irish Priests: Archbishop "Dagger John" Hughes

Probably no one better typifies the fierce determination to protect the Irish than Fr. John Hughes. Born in County Tyrone, Hughes emigrated early to the U.S. with his family, settling in Chambersburg, Pennsylvania with his parents and brother. He wanted to be a priest but was rejected by the seminary in Emmitsburg, Maryland repeatedly, finally getting hired as a gardener.

According to Fordham University, it was Elizabeth Anne Bayley Seton (now St. Elizabeth Seton) who got him into seminary. It's hard to imagine what might have happened to American Catholics had he not been accepted.

He began his career in Philadelphia but eventually was transferred to New York, where he founded Fordham University. He then became bishop of New York, a diocese that included the entire state and stretched west into New Jersey.

Somewhere along the line, Hughes earned the nickname "Dagger John." Perhaps this was because he carried on fiery written debates with Protestant clerics over the rights of Catholic schoolchildren to use a Catholic version of the Bible, or perhaps it was because he simply got things done on behalf of the Irish. Some scholars say that it was because when he signed his name, he drew a little cross with a dagger base beside it. Whatever the reason, Hughes was a first-rate debater and fiery activist.

He decided that if the public schools were not going to accommodate Catholic children, then it was necessary to start Catholic schools, and so he did. He founded churches, Catholic social clubs, Catholic orphanages, Catholic hospitals, and Catholic labor unions, starting all of this growth as early as 1850 while famine immigrants were still pouring into America.

As New York went, so went the nation, and by 1900, there were 12,000 parishes in America and more than 3,300 Catholic schools, with more than 50,000 nuns teaching and working in these institutions! By 1890, there were more than seven million Irish in America, most of them being served by and participating in the parish life of the Catholic Church.

Although Catholic schools are now closing all over America, having peaked in the 1960s when more than 13,000 schools enrolled 5 million students, there are still 6,500 in existence, serving almost 2 million students.

In 1844, when Philadelphia exploded into violence, Hughes was afraid that the riots would spread to New York. He gave the mayor of New York a warning, saying that if one Catholic church was burned, New York would become another Moscow (which had been burned down in 1812 under Napoleon). Then he armed several thousand members of his congregations and stationed them at all the church doors. No church was burned!

In 1858, Hughes decided that it was important for the Irish to have a great American cathedral, and in that year, he laid the cornerstone of St. Patrick's Cathedral in New York, saying, "The spiritual descendants of St. Patrick have been outcasts from their native land and have been scattered over the earth. And though there may be no mark to designate the graves in which they slumber, still, the churches which they have erected are the most fitting headstones to commemorate the honorable history of the Irish people."

It took twenty-one years of building and fundraisers to open the cathedral, by which time

St. Patrick's Cathedral sketch, 1890. (Library of Congress Digital Collection)

Bishop Hughes had died. One of the most interesting facts about the original cathedral is that is was raised without its spires, which were added over the next nine years. The location was considered the "wilderness," and the establishment called the construction "Hughes' Folly," but the bishop would not be stopped, and that may be a metaphor for the rise of our ancestors. Hughes is buried in the cathedral.

Irish-American Higher Education

In addition to churches and schools, Hughes' founding of Fordham signified a proliferation of Catholic universities and colleges throughout the United States. As of this writing, there are more than 250 Catholic institutions of higher education in America, ranging from small liberal-arts colleges to giant heavyhitters such as Notre Dame, Villanova, Boston College, Catholic University of America, Georgetown, and Marquette.

The legacy of Catholic schools in America is that our ancestors came to understand that education was the way up and out of their modest circumstances. By 2010, more than 40 million of us claim Irish ancestry, 90 percent of us hold high-school degrees, and more than 30 percent of us hold bachelor's degrees or higher. That means almost 13 million Irish-Americans are college or graduate-school educated!

21

Meanwhile Back at the Ranch: Rising Irish and Bold Fenian Men

Many scholars think that when Thomas Francis Meagher and Michael Corcoran recruited men to fight in the Civil War, they were also training men to return to Ireland to fight against Britain, as both had been members of secret societies before they left (or were thrown out of) Ireland.

In fact, America was full of secret Irish societies who were bent on setting Ireland free, especially in the early days of immigration. Some of these included:

- The Ancient Order of Hibernians
- The Fenian Brotherhood
- Clan na Gael
- A trilogy of societies named for St. Patrick

Most of these societies arose out of organizations such as the Ribbonmen or United Irishmen, who had waged secret wars against British rule during the landlord/tenant period in Ireland.

You will remember the Ancient Order of Hibernians from our discussion of the Molly Maguires. Founded in Ireland, AOH was particularly active in Ulster. The first American branches were founded in 1836 in New York and Pottsville, Pennsylvania, and an early goal was to defend the churches of Philadelphia and New York from the nativist Know-Nothing groups that we discussed earlier.

Eventually they became involved, according to most historians, in helping the Molly Maguires to resist the mine owners of Pennsylvania, and they were staunch supporters of the Easter Rising (more about that in a minute).

The Fenian Brotherhood has a long anti-British history. The United

Irishmen of the late 1700s evolved into the Young Irelanders of the 1840s (the organization to which Thomas Francis Meagher belonged). When Meagher was sent to Australia, two other members, James Stephens and John O'Mahony, escaped to France. Later, O'Mahony came to America and founded the Fenian Brotherhood in 1858. Stephens eventually sneaked back into Ireland and founded the Irish Revolutionary Brotherhood, later called the Irish Republican Brotherhood (IRB), from which the Easter Rising would arise.

In America, the Fenian Brotherhood began to raise money for the IRB in Ireland. Now, for a moment, we will hearken all the way back to part 1 of this book. You will remember the Fenians, the warrior army of ancient Ireland. O'Mahony named his secret American army after that organization. Believe it or not, thousands of Irish immigrants joined the Fenian Brotherhood, many of them soldiers who had fought in the American Civil War.

They organized themselves into cells, eventually dividing into two different groups. In one of the strangest twists of history ever, the groups decided that the best course of action for freeing Ireland was to invade Canada!

Yes, you read that right: invade Canada.

To us, from this distance, this plan has the ring of a *Saturday Night Live* skit, but perhaps from their perspective, it was their closest access to the British government.

One "force," led by O'Mahony with some seven hundred Fenians, tried to invade New Brunswick and take over Canada's Campobello Island. They were defeated by the British Navy.

The second force was led by Irish-born Capt. John O'Neill, who had commanded the Seventh Colored Infantry during the American Civil War. In June of 1866, he took a group of about the same size, crossed the Niagara River, and occupied Fort Erie. Believe it or not, O'Neill and his Civil War veterans were successful in two battles in Canada, defeating two groups of British troops before retreating back to the U.S. That success led to another invasion in 1870, for which O'Neill was arrested, but he was later pardoned by Ulysses S. Grant.

In fact, the U.S. government may have known about these raids beforehand and did very little but wink at them after the fact, because there was no love lost with England, both historically and because England had not supported the Union during the American Civil War.

Although the whole venture seems . . . well . . . silly to us from this remove, it was anything but to the Fenian Brotherhood and it may well have added fuel to the Irish Republican movement in Ireland.

Eventually, in 1867, when the two American factions of the Fenian Brotherhood could not resolve their differences and unite, the organization known as Clan na Gael arose with the same goals as the previous organizations: Irish freedom from Britain.

Today the strongest Irish society still extant in America is the Ancient Order of Hibernians, which boasts more than 100,000 members between its men's and women's divisions. It is now an Irish-Catholic organization that promotes Irish culture and participates in many charitable efforts throughout the country. Many notable Americans such as Pres. John F. Kennedy and Bishop Fulton Sheen have been modern members of the AOH.

The Easter Rising of 1916

To discuss the Easter Rising with any degree of scholarly depth would require an entire book and indeed, numerous tomes have been written on the subject. For the purposes of our discussion here, we will sketch the events of the Irish Rebellion but focus on what it meant for America in terms of immigration and our ongoing relationship with Ireland.

During Easter Week of 1916, four insurrection groups—the Irish Republican Brotherhood, Citizens Army, Irish Volunteers, and Cumann na mBan (the women's army)—took over several locations in Dublin, including the General Post Office on O'Connell Street, the Four Courts, and St. Stephen's Green, among others.

With a tiny force of less than 1,500 people, they held their positions until the British sent over reinforcements from England later in the week. Most of the leaders were captured at that time and imprisoned, but during the week, those leaders managed to publish a declaration of independence called the *Poblacht na h'Eireann*, proclaiming the Irish Republic free of Great Britain.

In the way of previous Irish rebellions, this one was put down by the British. Many Irish people did not know that the Rising was taking place, as it occurred almost exclusively in Dublin, and when they discovered it, even many Dubliners did not support it because it was causing damage and death throughout the city. It might have disappeared like previous rebellions, but the British government executed all of the signers of the declaration and a number of other leaders of the rebellion at Kilmainham Jail.

The executions made martyrs of men who might otherwise have faded from the history of Irish rebellions, and a war for Irish independence began in earnest, led by the Irish Republican Army (IRA) under Michael Collins and heavily supported with both money and arms by Irish organizations in the United States.

Executed After the Rising

Eamon Ceannt	Signer
Thomas Clarke	Signer
Conn Colbert	
James Connolly	Signer
Edward Daly	
Sean Heuston	
Michael Mallon	
Sean MacBride	
Sean MacDiarmada	Signer
Thomas MacDonagh	Signer
Michael O'Hanrahan	
Patrick Pearse	Signer
William Pearse	
Joseph Mary Plunkett	Signer

Éamon de Valera, one of the leaders of the Rising, was spared execution because he had been born in America to an immigrant mother from Limerick. In 1919, he was elected president of the newly formed Dáil Éireann (the Irish Parliament) and sent to America to try to win recognition there for an Irish Republic. While he did not get satisfaction for that quest, Irish-American organizations managed to raise more than five million dollars for the war for Irish independence!

Eventually, in a long war of attrition, the Irish wore the British down and Michael Collins, Arthur Griffith, and Robert Barton were sent to London to negotiate a treaty. Called the Irish Free State Treaty, it was ratified by the Dáil Éireann in January of 1922 and supported by most of the people of Ireland, but it split the newly formed government down the middle because it left the six counties of the North in English control and required an oath of fealty to Britain.

The result was a terrible civil war between the Irish themselves that lasted from 1922 to 1923, split the fighters for freedom in half, and ruined the friendship of Michael Collins and Éamon de Valera. For a brilliant look at this civil war, Neil Jordan's movie *Michael Collins*, though it contains some speculative elements, is evocative and sad.

American reaction to the Irish civil war ranged, by and large, from disbelief to disappointment. Most historians say that it caused a significant drop in the memberships in radicalized Irish-American organizations when the Irish started fighting among themselves.

Ireland was declared a republic in 1949, with complete independence from Britain, but the Irish civil war did not really end until the late 1990s. It had continued on in Northern Ireland in the skirmishes between the forces of the IRA) and Great Britain euphemistically known as the "Troubles."

At right, the "Troubles" are portrayed on a wall in Derry, Northern Ireland.

Once again, the strong link between Ireland and America was evidenced throughout this period, as Pres. Bill Clinton visited Ireland, made phone calls to both parties, and sent Sen. George Mitchell to Ireland to help to negotiate a truce in Northern Ireland.

Eventually, despite sectarian violence on both sides, the talks resulted in the Good Friday Accords in April of 1998 and a diminution of violence in Northern Ireland after hundreds of years.

22

Diaspora

All of our ancestors' trials and sorrows, invasions and starvations, have resulted in perhaps the most widely dispersed population in the history of the world.

- More than 4 million Canadians are of Irish lineage, about 12 percent in a population of over 35 million.
- More than 7 million people are ancestrally Irish in Australia, a whopping 30 percent of their population of 24 million.
- In the 2011 British census, a little more than 400,000 residents of Britain were Irish born, out of a population of 64 million. Most estimates say that about 5-6 million living in Britain are of recent Irish ancestry, by virtue of a parent or grandparent, but a whopping 14 million *claim* to be of Irish lineage.
- But by far, Irish-Americans are the largest slice of the diaspora pie, with more than 40 million of us in an overall population of 316 million. And while that number constitutes 13 percent of the U.S. population, it does not count the more than 4 million people who claimed Scots-Irish ancestry on the most recent census!

It is interesting to note that other populations who migrated to America often returned to their home countries. For example, scholars estimate that more than half of all Greek immigrants and nearly half of all Italian immigrants eventually returned. Not so with the Irish; there was no home to return to. Fewer than 7 percent of the Irish ever returned, higher only than American Jews, who also did not return.

From the 1700s until now, nearly 10 million people left Ireland. Its population never returned to its pre-Famine levels and even today rests at about 4.5 million.

Several modern waves of immigration from Ireland to America occurred—one after the Rising and the Irish civil war, a second one in the 1950s when the Irish economy was in tatters, and a third in the 1980s when many Irish were forced into illegal-alien status by a poor economy at home and immigration limits here.

A new wave of highly educated young Irish people are, even at this writing, boarding airplanes and setting their caps for Amerikay. You will meet them in New York City and Philadelphia. They will be students in your classroom and guests in your home. They may be your relatives.

Wish them *fáilte,* brothers and sisters, *fáilte* ("welcome"). For they are here among their American cousins. We will know them by their faces and their voices, the rhythm of their speech, and the stories we will tell each other. We will know them in the deep genetic river of our ancestry, Irish at the marrow, carrying the story in our bones, in our very bones.

For Further Reading: An Annotated Bibliography

Nonfiction

Callahan, Bob, ed. *The Big Book of American Irish Culture.* New York: Penguin, 1987.

This book is pure fun, lavishly illustrated, and organized around outlaws, politicians, hoofers, and even such subjects as Irish-themed Sunday "funnies."

Coffey, Michael, and Terry Golway. *The Irish in America.* New York: Hyperion, 1997.

This lavish, well-organized book covers the famine immigration and the subsequent Irish rise through hard labor, parish life, politics, theater, and education.

Coogan, Tim Pat. *The Man Who Made Ireland: The Life and Times of Michael Collins.* New York: Roberts Rinehart, 1992.

Oh what a fascinating and sad book this is. Michael Collins was the leader of the Irish revolution against Great Britain and the negotiator of the Free State Treaty that led, unfortunately, to the Irish Civil War. Coogan brings Collins so completely to life that you will believe you have met him.

——. *Wherever Green Is Worn: The Story of the Irish Diaspora.* New York: Palgrave, 2000.

Brilliant Irish historian Coogan covers Irish immigration, largely forced, to Britain, Australia, New Zealand, Africa, the Caribbean, Latin America, Asia, and, of course, Canada and the United States.

Daniels, Roger. *Coming to America: A History of Immigration and Ethnicity in American Life.* New York: Harper Perennial, 1990.

Daniels breaks down the consecutive waves of immigrants from all over the world, with the Irish migrations being just a few sections of the book. He does a very good job of differentiating the reasons and times for each migration, and the reasons that drove each group of immigrants to American shores are varied and fascinating.

Fanning, Charles. *The Irish Voice in America: 250 Years of Irish-American Fiction.* 2nd ed. Lexington: University of Kentucky Press, 2000.

Fanning's book examines in detail all of the fiction on the Irish-American experience beginning in the 1800s and coming up to the turn of this century. He unpacks both style and theme and relates each author's works to the larger context of the immigrant and post-immigrant Irish experience.

Glazer, Nathan, and Daniel Patrick Moynihan. *Beyond the Melting Pot: The Negroes, Puerto Ricans, Jews, Italians and Irish of New York City.* 2nd ed. Cambridge: MIT Press, 1976.

This is a most unusual book, with each chapter assessing one of the titular ethnic groups and its current and past importance and influence in New York City. What makes it odd is that it conflates facts with opinion, predicting the future relevance of each group based upon its present position. History becomes prognostication in ways that, in the case of the Irish, have not proven to be true. For example, two of the oddest assertions are that the New York Irish have never risen above their working-class roots nor produced an intellectual class of writers and thinkers. This is particularly odd when one assumes that Daniel Patrick Moynihan had a heavy hand in the Irish chapter.

Griffin, William D. *The Book of Irish Americans.* New York: Three Rivers Press, 1990.

You can read this book from cover to cover or choose to dip in and out, as it is filled with short pieces illustrating the life of some fascinating character or event in Irish-American history.

Logue, Paddy. *Being Irish.* Dublin: Oak Tree Press, 2000.

This is a series of short essays by a wide variety of Irish and

Irish-American notables, each analyzing what it means to be Irish, dwell in Ireland, be Protestant in Ireland, be part of the diaspora, etc.

Lynch-Brennan, Margaret. *The Irish Bridget: Irish Immigrant Women in Domestic Service in America, 1840-1930.* Syracuse: Syracuse University Press, 2014.
Using photographs and epistolary sources, Lynch-Brennan makes the Irish "Bridgets" or "Biddies" come to life as feisty, funny, determined, and brave. This is an academic source but very accessible.

Maier, Thomas. *The Kennedys: America's Emerald Kings.* New York: Perseus, 2003.
This huge tome gives real insight into the Kennedy family, how they came to power, their spectacular access to both secular and church leaders, and the details of their political campaigns and terms. One particularly interesting section explains how John F. Kennedy and Pope John XXIII changed America's perception of Catholics, making them far less frightening and therefore much less subject to prejudice.

McCaffrey, Lawrence J. *The Irish Catholic Diaspora in America.* Washington, D.C.: Catholic University of America Press, 1984.
Scholarly and at the same time wonderfully anecdotal, this study examines the terrible prejudice toward Catholic Irish immigrants and the necessary social and political structures that arose to combat that prejudice and reconfigure Irish-Americans into upwardly mobile and highly educated Americans.

McNamara, Julia, ed. *The Irish Face in America.* New York: Bullfinch Press, 2004.
Organized around the trope of the classic Irish face, this gorgeous coffee-table book features both famous Irish-Americans in politics, sports, theater, movies, and culture as well as lesser-known but fascinating ones.

Morris, Charles R. *American Catholic: The Saints and Sinners Who Built America's Most Powerful Church.* New York: Vintage Books, 1997.
This is a riveting study of the American Catholic Church, its history, and its character, written with the skill of a novelist but hewing to the

record. Morris does a masterful job of articulating how and why the American Catholic character became so different from the European Catholic character. He roots those conclusions in the thoroughly Irish development of a Church that was anti-authoritarian and political by virtue of the famine immigrants it served, first Irish and then later Italian and Eastern European. Every American Catholic should read this book.

Whalen, William J. *The Irish in America.* Chicago: Claretian, 1972.
　　This monograph focuses on famous Irish-Americans.

Video—Documentaries

The Irish in America. DVD. Directed by Thomas Lennon and Mark Zwonitzer. A&E Home Video, 2013.
　　Narrated by Aidan Quinn, this lovely documentary crosses the ocean between Ireland and America to explain and illustrate the successive waves of Irish immigrants and how they made their way in the new country.

Out of Ireland. DVD. Directed by Paul Wagner. Shanachie Entertainment with funding from the National Endowment for the Humanities, 1997.
　　This documentary, narrated by Kelly McGillis, focuses on the prejudice against Irish Catholics in America and on the jobs and political maneuvers that the Irish used to climb the immigrant ladder.

Video—Features and Miniseries

Far and Away. DVD. Directed by Ron Howard. Universal Pictures, 1992.
　　Starring Tom Cruise and Nicole Kidman and as "schlocky" a movie as ever hit the big screen, the scenery is nonetheless beautiful, though the Irish accents are not. The backstory is of a young Irish immigrant who becomes a bare-knuckle boxer and then immigrates to Oklahoma during the land rush.

The Fighting 69th. DVD. Directed by William Keighley. Warner Brothers, 1940.

This World War I moral fable starring James Cagney and Pat O'Brien is about an all-Irish New York regiment that has existed since the Civil War.

Gangs of New York. DVD. Directed by Martin Scorsese. Miramax, 2002.

Five Points is the notorious New York slum where urban Irish immigrants lived after the famine Migration, and Scorsese's portrayal of the hatred of the Nativists for the immigrants, especially the Irish, is accurate. The movie, starring Daniel Day-Lewis and Leonardo DiCaprio, will give viewers a feel for the conditions in which our ancestors were trapped if their post-famine migration was urban.

Going My Way. DVD. Directed by Leo McCarey. Paramount Pictures, 1944.

American prejudice against Catholics began to dissipate with films like this, in which loveable, affable Irish-American priest Father O'Malley, played by Bing Crosby, stands for wisdom, humor, and a moral center for lost youth. Its sequel *The Bells of St. Mary's* was released by RKO in 1946 and adds Ingrid Bergman to the cast, as a nun who helps Father O'Malley build a parish school.

The Last Hurrah. DVD. Directed by John Ford. Columbia Pictures, 1958.

Ford studies here an old-fashioned Irish politician, played by Spencer Tracy, and the charm and corruption of that system.

The Manions of America. DVD. Directed by Charles Dubin. First released in 1981. Entertainment One, 2012.

This television miniseries starring Pierce Brosnan and Kate Mulgrew was penned by famed soap-opera writer Agnes Nixon, so it has many five-handkerchief moments with swelling violins, but it portrays a young tenant who emigrates to America during the Irish famine, serves in the American Civil War, and makes his way to wealth, along the way marrying his landlord's daughter. The scenery is beautiful on both sides of the water, but Brosnan does a very good job of portraying the heart-wrenching separation from Ireland.

The Molly Maguires. DVD. Directed by Martin Ritt. Paramount
   Pictures, 1970.

Historians differ on whether or not the Molly Maguires were an
organized resistance group, a terrorist group, or a group at all, but
this film starring Sean Connery and Richard Harris focuses on the
divided loyalties of Pinkerton detective James MacParland, who is
tasked with infiltrating the group (under the name James MacKenna)
and bringing it down. The movie was filmed in true Pennsylvania
coal country around Eckley and Jim Thorpe.

The Sullivans. DVD. Directed by Lloyd Bacon. Twentieth Century Fox,
   1944.

Starring Anne Baxter, this is based on the sad, true story of five
brothers who signed up together to serve in the U.S. Navy during
World War II and died together in the Pacific theater. The story of
the Sullivans caused the armed forces to change their policies about
brothers serving in the same companies and theaters during wartime.

Yankee Doodle Dandy. DVD. Directed by Michael Curtiz. Warner
   Brothers, 1942.

Called "the man who owned Broadway," George Cohan was an
Irish-American (original name Keohane) who spent his childhood
in a vaudeville act called "The Four Cohans" and grew up to write
hundreds of songs and produce Broadway shows. Once you watch
this biopic, you will watch it again and again, as fellow Irish-American
Jimmy Cagney brings a twinkling, high-Irish energy to his portrayal
of Cohan, and his legendary nasal voice makes Cohan's songs equally
memorable.

Appendix

Irish-American Writers and Entertainers

Irish-American Writers

1920s
- **F. Scott Fitzgerald.** Examined American wealth and consumerism in *The Great Gatsby.*
- **Eugene O'Neill.** Pulitzer Prize-winning playwright of such plays as *Desire Under the Elms* and *Long Day's Journey into Night.*

1930s
- **James T. Farrell.** Examined the effects of the Great Depression on the Chicago Irish in the Studs Lonigan Trilogy.
- **Margaret Mitchell.** Author of *Gone with the Wind.*
- **John O'Hara.** Author of *Appointment in Samarra, Butterfield 8,* and *Pal Joey,* which became a Broadway musical.

1940s
- **Mary Coyle Chase.** Author of *Harvey,* the wonderful play about a man and his imaginary(?) rabbit friend.

1950s-70s
- **Flannery O'Connor.** Southern Gothic short-story and novel writer of Irish Catholic sensibilities. Won the National Book Award for her collected short stories.
- **John Kennedy Toole.** Committed suicide before being awarded the Pulitzer Prize for *A Confederacy of Dunces* in 1981.

Modern
- **Jimmy Breslin.** Pulitzer Prize-winning journalist with the *New York Daily News.*
- **Lisa Carey.** Author of *The Mermaids Singing* and *In the Country of the Young,* magical-realist novels heavily influenced by Irish mythology.
- **Tom Clancy.** Author of numerous Jack Ryan thrillers. Died in 2013.
- **Mary Higgins Clark.** American writer of more than forty bestselling mystery and suspense novels.
- **Pat Conroy.** Author of *The Prince of Tides* and *The Water Is Wide,* the latter a beautiful tale of teaching among the Gullah children on pre-resort Daufuskie Island.

- **Thomas Flanagan.** Author of numerous Irish novels, including *The Year of the French* and *The Tenants of Time.* Died in 2002.
- **Mary Gordon.** Author of numerous novels, essays, and memoirs, most notably *Final Payments,* a novel utterly rooted in the dual swords of Catholic guilt and Catholic devotion to family.
- **Andrew Greeley.** Courageous and controversial Irish Catholic priest, sociologist, and novelist whose work censured the Church for child abuse and hypocrisy and advocated for a theology of the passionate love of God for humans. Died in 2013.
- **Pete Hamill.** Journalist for the *New York Post* and the *New York Daily News* and author of nonfiction and fiction books. Has the uncanny ability to capture the world in words that are both photographic and emotionally evocative.
- **William Kennedy.** Pulitzer Prize-winning author of *Ironweed* and the novels in the Albany Cycle, featuring the Irish Phelan family of Albany, New York.
- **Dennis Lehane.** Boston Irish author of *Mystic River, Gone Baby Gone,* and the eerie and startling *Shutter Island,* all of which have been made into movies.
- **Cormac McCarthy.** Pulitzer Prize-winning author of *The Road* and the gorgeous Border Trilogy.
- **Frank McCourt.** Pulitzer Prize-winning author of *Angela's Ashes.* Died in 2009.
- **Tim O'Brien.** Pulitzer Prize-winning author of *The Things They Carried.*
- **Anna Quindlen.** Pulitzer Prize-winning journalist for the *New York Times* and author of the novels *One True Thing, Black and Blue,* and *Blessings.*
- **Nora Roberts.** Bestselling romance and suspense writer.
- **John Patrick Shanley.** Playwright and winner of the Pulitzer Prize for *Doubt: A Parable,* which was made into a movie with Meryl Streep and Philip Seymour Hoffman.

Irish-American Poets	Irish-American Actors, Dancers, Directors	
Daniel Berrigan	Edward Burns	Denis Leary
Louise Bogan	Jimmy Cagney	Kate and Rooney
Billy Collins	George Clooney	Mara
Robert Creeley	Bing Crosby	Dylan McDermott
Robert Frost	Walt Disney	Bridget
Tess Gallagher	Jimmy Fallon	Moynahan
Robinson Jeffers	Michael Flatley	Kate Mulgrew
XJ Kennedy	John Ford	Conan O'Brien
Galway Kinnell	Helen Hayes	Chris O'Donnell
Thomas Lynch	Gene Kelly	Aidan Quinn
Frank O'Hara	Grace Kelly	Spencer Tracy

Afterword

This book is not intended to be a scholarly treatise. I have been teaching Irish diaspora, mythology, literature for more than two decades and have never been able to find a single book that does what I want it to do—fly like a space capsule high above the long sweep of Irish and Irish-American history and show my students the map from space.

There are two ways to write a nonfiction book: 1) dive deep into the well of the subject and give readers all of the particulars and provenances or 2) skim like a stone on the surface of a lake and show readers all of the important events. I was searching for a big-picture book.

In the course of that search I read hundreds of scholarly books on single subjects: books on the druids, books on Michael Collins, books on Oliver Cromwell, books on Irish women in domestic service in America. All of them have been fascinating but all of them have been single-subject specific.

Because I could not find what I wanted in that long search, I decided to write it. I set as my guiding principles four essential goals:

- To select from all of the scholarly books I have read the highlights of our history and focus not on the details but on the big picture: *This happened then and because it happened, this resulted*.
- To keep the focus on us as Irish-Americans in every possible way: Who were our most ancient of ancestors? How have they influenced us genetically and ideologically? How did we get here? What happened to push us out of Ireland? What beliefs and customs did we come with? What did we do once we got here?
- To make the experience of reading this book as much like my classroom as I possibly could. My classroom is full of images and sounds. It is full of storytelling—constant storytelling. To accomplish those goals I used photographs and my artist daughter drew complex Celtic designs. I broke the text up with sidebars and used fictional or mythological storytelling wherever I could to illustrate a point.
- To make this book accessible to a very specific group of readers: Irish-American citizens and students who are interested in learning about the full and fascinating scope of their story in as engaging a format as possible. My hope is that this book will appeal to the browser in the bookstore or the student in the introductory Irish studies course.

Whenever I write a book, I learn something about myself. In the writing of this book I learned that my family's journey is and was the archetypal Irish journey. I suppose I always knew that, but organizing this book put their journey firmly in the timeline.

The bulk of my 1800s great-grandparents were Famine Irish, most from County Mayo, most emigrating to America in the worst years of the Famine and then for several years afterward, as they sent back for brothers and sisters at home.

They were Catholic; some of them lived in a ghetto behind a cathedral in a steel-mill town. They worked the mill and the railroads and the coalmines and were extremely tight-lipped and secretive about their origins. I imagine they worked hard to get rid of the brogue, to dress American and eat American and become American. Parish life was, of course, everything—full belonging and protection from the terrors of the New World.

Along the way their names were changed from Irish monikers such as O'Manion and Ceannadaigh to Manning and Kennedy.

Like many of our ancestors they figured out very early that education was the ticket, the key to breaking the code. My grandmother managed, on her own and in hotel service, to put two daughters through college. I am named for her. Both of her daughters were teachers and she would be so proud that I teach at a Catholic college.

None of them ever returned to Ireland—not once, not ever. I was the first person and the first generation to return. I have returned again and again and again, taking my students to Ireland, doing my graduate work in Ireland, learning to speak Irish and read Irish and carry the stories in my head and my heart and on my tongue. All of my ancestors go "home" with me.

When the Famine ship *Jeanie Johnston* came to Philadelphia, I went to the dock with my Irish novels in my arms. The captain, a perceptive sort of fellow, looked at the pile and asked, "You wrote these, did you?" I nodded, my heart hammering. He reached out his hands. "And you want me to sail your people home?" I placed the books in his outstretched hands.

I am so grateful to my ancestors that they had *that* much courage, that they worked and fought and scrabbled, that they sacrificed to get their whole family educated, that they chose a country where I can be a strong, highly educated, proud, American-Irish woman.

All my life I have tried to imagine them getting off the boat, their own hearts hammering, some in New York, some in Quebec. I have tried to imagine the hunger and the fear and the strangeness of it all. I wonder what it was like to be the lowest of the low in American society, something not quite human, knowing all the while that you were carrying inside you all the stories, all the faith, all the stubbornness, and all the magic in the world.

For that is what we carry. "We are the music-makers," said poet Arthur O'Shaughnessy. "And we are the dreamers of dreams." And so we are. Our ancestors carried us here; they gave us their dreams and their songs and their faith. We owe it to them to carry it on.

Bail O Dhia ar an obair.
Bless, O God, the work.

Index